Quotes
That
Breathe

Compiled and edited by Dennis van Westerborg

Whimprint Books

Library and Archives Canada Cataloguing in Publication

Quotes That Breathe / compiled and edited by Dennis van Westerborg
ISBN 978-0-9735300-4-9 (paperback)

1.Authors--Quotations. I. van Westerborg, Dennis, 1930-, editor
PN6081.V35 2016   082   C2016-904084-4

INTRODUCTION

This collection is not another Bartlett's, if only because I have included many unfamiliar, yet poignant, quotes from 337 authors, marshalled under 32 headings.

What makes my compilation special is a hefty injection of trenchant observations I have mined as a lifelong student of Emerson and Thoreau from some 15,000 pages of their journals - material not readily found anywhere else.

Dennis van Westerborg

AUTHORS QUOTED

Henry Adams (1838 - 1918)
Thomas Adams (fl.1640)
Joseph Addison (1672 - 1719)
Scipio Africanus (234 - 183 BC)
Abul-'Ala al-Ma'arri (973 - 1057)
Mary Allen (1810 - 82)
Frédéric Amiel (1821 - 81)
Anacharsis (6th cent. BC)
Abdullah Ansari (1006 - 89)
Susan B. Anthony (1820 - 1906)
St. Thomas Aquinas (1225 - 74)
Aristophanes (450 - 388 BC)
Bettina von Arnim (1785 - 1859)
Matthew Arnold (1822 - 88)
Athenaeus (2nd cent. AD)
St. Augustine (354 - 430)
Marcus Aurelius (121 - 80)
Francis Bacon (1561 - 1626)
A.J. Balfour (1848 - 1930)
John Balguy (1686 - 1748)
Hosea Ballou (1771 - 1852)
George Bancroft (1800 - 91)
Karl Barth (1886 - 1968)
H.W. Beecher (1813 - 87)
Beethoven (1770 - 1827)
Aphra Behn (1640 - 89)
Hilaire Belloc (1870 - 1953)
Nathaniel Benchley (1889 - 1945)
George Berkeley (1685 - 1753)
St. Bernard (923 - 1008)
Bias (6th cent.BC)
Josh Billings (1818 - 85)
Bion (2nd cent.BC)
Bismarck (1815 - 98)

R.D. Blackmore (1825 - 1900)
William Blake (1757 - 1827)
Boileau-Despréaux (1636 - 1711)
C.N. Bovée (1820 - 1904)
F.H. Bradley (1846 - 1924)
Phillips Brooks (1835 - 93)
Thomas Brooks (1608 - 80)
Sir Thomas Browne (1605 - 82)
Robert Browning (1812 - 89)
William Cullen Bryant (1794-1878)
Charles Buck (1771 - 1815)
Edmund Burke (1729 - 97)
Robert Burton (1577-1640)
Samuel Butler (1600 - 80)
Samuel Butler (1835 - 1902)
Lord Byron (1788 - 1824)
Callimachus (3rd cent.BC)
Thomas Campbell (1777 - 1844)
Thomas Carlyle (1795 - 1881)
William Cartwright (1611 - 43)
Cato the Elder (234 - 149 BC)
Richard Cecil (1748 - 77)
Thomas Chalmers (1780 - 1847)
S.R.N. Chamfort (1741 - 94)
W.E. Channing (1780 - 1842)
E.H. Chapin (1814 - 80)
G.K. Chesterton (1874 - 1936)
Chuang Tzu (369 - 286 BC)
Charles Churchill (1731 - 64)
Winston Churchill (1874 - 1965)
Cicero (106 - 43 BC)
E.H. Clarendon (1609 - 74)
Cleanthes (330 - 232 BC)
William Cobbett (1763 - 1835)

Hartley Coleridge (1796 - 1849)	Nathaniel Emmons (1745 - 1840)
S.T. Coleridge (1772 - 1834)	Epictetus (60 - 117)
Jeremy Collier (1650 - 1726)	Epicurus (341 - 270 BC)
C.C. Colton (1780 - 1832)	Euripides (480 - 406 BC)
August Comte (1798 - 1857)	George Farquhar (1678 - 1707)
William Congreve (1670 - 1729)	Madam Fée (fl. 1850)
Joseph Conrad (1857 - 1924)	Arthur Davidson Ficke (1883-1945)
Pierre Corneille (1606 - 84)	Firdusi (935 - 1020)
Abraham Cowley (1618 - 67)	Oscar W. Firkins (1864 - 1932)
William Cowper (1731 - 1800)	John Florio (1533 - 1625)
George Crabbe (1754- 1833)	La Fontaine (1621 - 95)
Saint Cyprian (200 -58)	B.C. Forbes (1880 - 1954)
Dante (1265 - 1321)	E.M. Forster (1879 - 1970)
William Henry Davies (1870 - 1940)	Benjamin Franklin (1706 - 90)
Daniel Defoe (1661 - 1731)	Thomas Fuller (1608 - 61)
William DeMorgan (1839 - 1917)	Dr. Thomas Fuller (1654 - 1734)
Thomas DeQuincey (1785 - 1859)	Salomon Ibn Gabirol (1020 - 70)
John Dewey (1859 - 1952)	Galen (129 - 99)
Wentworth Dillon (1633 - 85)	Garin (1205 - 50)
Diogenes (412 -323 BC)	John Gay (1688 - 1732)
Isaac D'Israeli (1766 - 1848)	Edward Gibbon (1737 - 94)
W. Macneile Dixon (1866 - 1946)	William Gilbert (1540 - 1603)
Henry Austin Dobson (1840 - 1921)	Joseph Glanvill (1636 - 80)
Sir Arthur Conan Doyle (1859-1930)	J.W. von Goethe (1749 - 1832)
John Dryden (1631 - 1700)	Oliver Goldsmith (1728 - 84)
A. Dumas (1802 - 70)	Baltasar Gracián (1601 - 58)
Émile Durkheim (1858 - 1917)	Thomas Gray (1716 - 71)
John Dyer (1700 - 58)	David Grayson (1870 - 1946)
Sherwood Eddy (1871 - 1963)	Robert Greene (1560 - 92)
R.C. (Bob) Edwards (1864 - 1922)	St. Gregory (330 - 89)
Tryon Edwards (1809 - 94)	Hafiz (1326 - 90)
Albert Einstein (1879 - 1955)	J.B.S. Haldane (1892 - 1964)
George Eliot (1819 - 80)	Arthur S. Hardy (1847 - 1930)
T.S. Eliot (1888 - 1965)	J.C. Hare (1796 - 1855)
Havelock Ellis (1859 - 1939)	and A.W. Hare (1792 - 1834)
R.W. Emerson (1803 - 82)	William Hazlitt (1778 - 1830)

Sir Arthur Helps (1813 - 75)
Lord Edward Herbert (1583 - 1648)
George Herbert (1593 - 1633)
J.G. Herder (1744 - 1803)
Hesiod (800 BC)
Hippocrates (460 - 377 BC)
A.A. Hodge (1823 - 86)
J.G. Holland (1819 - 81)
O.W. Holmes (1841 - 1935)
Homer (8th cent.BC)
Thomas Hood (1799 - 1845)
Gerard Manley Hopkins (1845 - 89)
George Horne (1730 - 92)
Nathaniel Howe (1764 - 1837)
Hsiang-Kuo (4th cent.BC)
Elbert Hubbard (1859 - 1915)
Victor Hugo (1802 - 85)
Anna M. Hülsemann (1853 - 1953)
Alexander von Humboldt (1769-1859)
David Hume (1711 - 76)
Leigh Hunt (1784 - 1859)
Saint Ignatius (35-107)
Dean Inge (1860 - 1954)
R.G. Ingersoll (1833 - 99)
Holbrook Jackson (1874 - 1948)
William James (1842 - 1910)
St. Jerome (342 - 420)
Douglas W. Jerrold (1803 - 57)
Samuel Johnson (1709 - 84)
Joseph Joubert (1754 - 1824)
Juvenal (60 - 140)
Nicos Kazantzakis (1883 - 1957)
John Keats (1795 - 1821)
Thomas á Kempis (1380 - 1471)
Charles F. Kettering (1876 - 1958)
John Maynard Keynes (1883 - 1946)

Hazrat Inayat Khan (1882 - 1927)
Sören Kierkegaard (1813 - 55)
Charles Kingsley (1819 - 75)
Rudyard Kipling (1865 - 1936)
Karl Kraus (1874 - 1936)
Karl C.F. Krause (1781 - 1832)
La Bruyère (1645 - 96)
La Rochefoucauld (1613 - 80)
Alphonse Lamartine (1790 - 1869)
Charles Lamb (1785 - 1834)
Letitia Elizabeth Landon (1802-38)
F.A. Lange (1828 - 75)
Lao Tzu (604 - 531 BC)
D.H. Lawrence (1885 - 1930)
Henry Sambrooke Leigh (1837-83)
Stanislaus Lezinsky (1677 - 1766)
Libanius (c.375)
Abraham Lincoln (1809 - 65)
John Locke (1632 - 1704)
H.W. Longfellow (1807 - 82)
J.R. Lowell (1819 - 91)
Lucan (39 - 65)
Lucian (117 - 80)
Lucretius (98 - 55 BC)
Maurice Maeterlinck (1862 - 1948)
N. de Malebranche (1638-1715)
Christopher Marlowe (1564 - 93)
Horace Mann (1796 - 1859)
D.R.P. Marquis (1878 - 1937)
Martial (40 - 112)
Andrew Marvell (1621 - 78)
Philip Massinger (1583 - 1640)
W. Somerset Maugham (1874-1965)
Guy de Maupassant (1850 - 93)
Elsa Maxwell (1883 - 1963)
H.L. Mencken (1880 - 1956)

Owen Meredith (1831 - 91)	Beilby Porteus (1731 - 1808)
Hugh H. Miller (1802 - 56)	Hiram Powers (1805 - 73)
John Milton (1608 - 74)	Matthew Prior (1664 - 1721)
Molière (1622 - 73)	Pythagoras (580 - 500 BC)
Montaigne (1533 - 92)	Francis Quarles (1592 - 1644)
Montesquieu (1689 - 1755)	Rabelais (1495 - 1553)
Dwight Moody (1837 - 99)	Lizette W. Reese (1856 - 1935)
Thomas Moore (1780 - 1852)	Madame Ricconboni (1713 - 92)
Hannah More (1745 - 1833)	Jean Paul Richter (1763 - 1825)
William Motherwell (1797 - 1835)	Rainer Maria Rilke (1875 - 1926)
Yusuf Nabi (Turkish poet, 1642-1712)	Joseph Ritson (1752 - 1803)
Cardinal Newman (1801 - 90)	Charles G.D. Roberts (1860 - 1943)
Sir Isaac Newton (1642 - 1727)	F.W. Robertson (1816 - 53)
Friedrich Nietzsche (1844 - 1900)	Theodore Roethke (1908 - 63)
Anaïs Nin (1903 - 77)	Samuel Rogers (1763 - 1855)
John Oldham (1600 - 36)	J.J. Rousseau (1712 - 78)
George Orwell (1903 - 50)	Helen Rowland (1875 - 1950)
Sir William Osler (1849 - 1919)	John Ruskin (1819 - 1900)
Ovid (43 BC - 17 AD)	Saadi (1184 - 1292)
Thomas Paine (1737 - 1809	Carl Sandburg (1878 - 1964)
Theodore Parker (1810 - 60)	James Sanford (1576)
Blaise Pascal (1623 - 62)	George Santayana (1863 - 1952)
Thomas Love Peacock (1785 - 1866)	Sir Walter Scott (1771 - 1832)
William Penn (1644 - 1718)	John Selden (1584 - 1654)
Petronius (1st cent.AD)	Seneca (2 BC - 65 AD)
William Lyon Phelps (1865 - 1943)	Shakespeare (1564 - 1616)
Philolaus (5th cent. BC)	Percy Bysshe Shelley (1792 - 1822)
Phocion (402 - 317 BC)	Frances Sheridan (1724 - 66)
Plato (428 - 347 BC)	Sir Charles Sherrington (1861-1952)
Plautus (254 - 184 BC)	William Gilmore Simms (1806 - 70)
Pliny the Elder (23 - 79)	Christopher Smart (1722 - 71)
Pliny the Younger (62 - 113)	Alexander Smith (1830 - 67)
Plutarch (46 - 120)	Socrates (469 - 399 BC)
Edgar Allen Poe (1809 - 49)	Sophocles (495 - 405 BC)
Polybius (205 - 125 BC)	Robert Southey (1774 - 1843)
Alexander Pope (1688 - 1744)	Herbert Spencer (1820 - 1903)

Oswald Spengler (1880 - 1936)
Spinoza (1632 - 77)
C.H. Spurgeon (1834 - 92)
Madame de Staël (1766 - 1817)
Laurence Sterne (1713 - 68)
R.L. Stevenson (1850 - 94)
R.S. Surtees (1803 - 64)
Madame Swetchine (1782 - 1857)
Jonathan Swift (1667 - 1745)
Publilius Syrus (1st cent.BC)
Tacitus (55 - 120)
Jeremy Taylor (1613 - 67)
Alfred Tennyson (1809 - 92)
Terence (195 - 159 BC)
St. Teresa of Avila (1515 - 82)
Thales (620 - 555 BC)
Themistocles (523 - 458 BC)
Francis Thompson (1859 - 1907)
James Thomson (1700 - 48)
H.D. Thoreau (1817 - 62)
Leo Tolstoy (1828 - 1910)
Richard C. Trench (1807- 86)
G.M. Trevelyan (1876 - 1962)
Martin Tupper (1810 - 89)
John Tyndall (1820 - 93)
Allan Updegraff (1883 - 1965)
Paul Valéry (1871 - 1945)
H.W. van Loon (1882 - 1944)
Varro (1st cent.AD)
Vauvenargues (1715 - 47)
Ralph Venning (1621 - 74)
Leonardo da Vinci (1452 - 1518)
Voltaire (1694 - 1778)
Edmund Waller (1605 - 87)
Horace Walpole (1717 - 97)
Benjamin Whichcote (1609 - 83)

E.P. Whipple (1819 - 86)
Henry Kirk White (1785 - 1806)
Walt Whitman (1819 - 92)
A.E. Wiggam (1871 - 1957)
Ella Wheeler Wilcox (1855 - 1919)
Oscar Wilde (1854 - 1900)
Alexander Wilson (1766 - 1813)
Johan de Witt (1625 - 72)
P.G. Wodehouse (1881 - 1925)
Christian von Wolff (1679 - 1754)
William Wordsworth (1770 - 1850)
Chauncey Wright (1830 - 75)
William Wycherley (1640 - 1716)
Xenophanes (570 - 480 BC)
Xenophon (430 - 355 BC)
Edward Young (1681 - 1765)
Israel Zangwill (1864 - 1926)
J.G. Zimmerman (1728 - 95)

SUBJECT HEADINGS

"Thoughts that breathe, and words that burn."

Thomas Gray (1716 - 71)

LIFE

Wodehouse: *What a queer thing life is! So unlike anything else....*

Anonymous graffito: *Life is a sexually transmitted disease.*

Pope: *This long disease, my life.*

Chamfort: *[Tragedy gives] too much importance to life and death.*

Haldane: *[Life] is something between mechanism and individuality, between chance and purpose.* (**Byron:** *...half dust, half deity.)*

Sherrington: *Individuality would seem to be through complexity an aim of life.*

Karl Kraus: *Life is an effort that deserves a better cause.*

Sherrington: *Life feeds on life....life is no sacred thing.*

G. Herbert: *Life is half spent before we know what it is.*

Butler (1902): *Life is the art of drawing sufficient conclusions from insufficient premises.*

Arnold: *Life has no moral purpose; no one is born with a duty to anyone else.*

Nabi: *Being is but a loan to us, and Life in trust we hold. [According to* **Locke** *the soul is that which is consciousness.]*

Lowell: *This life were brutish did we not sometimes/ Have intimation clear of wider scope.*

Africanus: *...the frailty of human life and the fickleness of fortune....*

Blake: *Man was made for joy and woe....*

Emerson: *The purpose of life seems to be to acquaint a man with himself.*

Tupper: *[Events] which aggravate thy soul today,/ May not meet again for centuries in the kaleidoscope of circumstance;/ For men and matters change, new elements mixing in continually. (***Tyndall:*** Life is a wave, which in no two consecutive moments of existence is composed of the same particles.)*

Kettering: *It is a man's destiny to ponder on the riddle of existence.*

Kierkegaard: *Life is not a problem to be solved but a reality to be experienced....Life can only be understood backwards, but it must be lived forwards.*

Goethe: *The object of life is life.*

Aurelius: *The universe is change; our life is what our thoughts make it....Do not then consider life a thing of any value. For look to the immensity of time behind you, and to the time which is before you.... (***Cowley:*** There are two sorts of eternity, from the Present backwards to Eternity, and from the Present forward.)*

Channing: *Life is a fragment, a moment between two eternities....*

DEATH and DYING

Young: *All men think all men mortal but themselves.*

Florio: *The end makes all men equal.*

De Morgan: *Death is only an incident in life.*

Johnson: *The act of dying is not of importance, it lasts so short a time.*

Spinoza: *A free man thinks of nothing less than death.*

Epicurus: *Death is nothing to us, since when we are, death has not come, and when death has come, we are not.*

Dryden: *Death in itself is nothing; but we fear/ To be we know not what; we know not where.*

Longfellow: *There is no Death! What seems so is transition....*

Aristophanes: *Who knows if death be life, and life be death.*

Plato: *...no one knows whether death, which they in their fear apprehend to be the greatest evil; may not be the greatest good.*

Lucan: *The gods conceal from the living how pleasant death is, so that they will continue to live.* (**Hawthorne:** *Providence seldom vouchsafes to mortals any more than just that degree of encouragement which suffices to keep them at reasonably full exertion of their powers.*)

Euripides: *Not to be born I count the same as death.* (**Hazlitt:** *To die is only to be as we were before we were born....* **Lucretius:** *We who are now are not concerned with ourselves in any previous existence....* **Cicero:** *Remove sensation and a man is exactly as though he had never been born.*)

Lucretius: *But even in sleep when mind and body alike are at rest, no one misses himself or sighs for life....* (**Byron:** *Death, so called, is a thing which makes men weep,/ And yet a third of life is passed in sleep.*)

Chuang Tzu: *That which has taken care of my birth is that which will take care of my death also.*

Latin proverb: *Live your own life, for you will die your own death.*

F. Thompson: *For we are born in other's pain,/ And perish in our own.*

Anaï's Nin: *People living deeply have no fear of death.*

Cicero: *I don't wish to die, but I care not if I were dead.* (**Martial:** *Neither to wish, nor fear to die....Neither dread your last day nor desire it.*)

Santayana: *The spiritual man resigns existence as gladly as he accepts it.* (**Unknown:** *There is pleasure enough in this life to make us wish to live, and pain enough to reconcile us to death when we can live no longer.*)

Johnson: *...life protracted is protracted woe.* (**Unknown:** *Our ability to prolong life outpaces our ability to make it worth living.*)

Pythagoras: *We are strangers in this world and the body is the tomb of the Soul, and yet that we are not to escape by self-murder, for we are the chattels of God.* (**Socrates:** *Man is a prisoner who has no right to open the door of his prison and run away....* **Cicero:** *The divinity who rules within us forbids us to quit this world without his command.*)

Lao Tzu: *If people do not fear death, what good is there in using death as a deterrent?*

SICKNESS, SUFFERING, PAIN

Sir A. Helps: *Experience is the extract of suffering.*

Euripides: *Suffering for mortals is nature's iron law.*

Seneca: *We suffer more in imagination than in reality.* (**S.T. Coleridge:** *Real pain can alone cure us of imaginary ills.*)

Butler (1680): *Our pains are real things, but all/ Our pleasures but fantastical.*

Cicero: *Pain is generally light if long, and short if severe.*

Saadi: *When belly with bad pains doth swell,/ It matters nought what else goes well.*

Thoreau: *'Tis healthy to be sick sometimes.*
  Sickness should not be allowed to extend further than the body.

Pliny the Elder: *In sickness the mind reflects upon itself.* (**Dr. Fuller:** *Sickness tells us what we are.*)

Proverb: *Affliction and adversity make men better.*

Meredith: *Sorrow humanizes our race.* (**Franklin:** *After crosses and losses men grow humbler and wiser....Calamity and prosperity are the touchstones of integrity.*)

Seneca: *A man in distress is a sacred thing.*

Bruyère: *The sight of certain miseries makes one ashamed of being happy.*

Petronius: *A physician is only a consoler of the mind.*

Milton: *Apt words have power to suage/ The tumors of a troubled mind.*

Burton: *Who lives medically, lives miserably.* (**Unknown:** *He who lives by prescription lives wretchedly.*)

Hubbard: *The worst about medicine is that one kind makes another necessary.*

Dean Inge: *A common error in our day is horror at the symptoms and neglect of the disease.*

GRIEF

Cleanthes: *...grief is an irrational contraction of the soul. (***Cicero:** *Grief is not natural but a matter of belief or opinion.* **Emerson:** *The only thing grief has taught me is to know how shallow it is.)*

Dillon: *As men that truly grieve at funerals/ Are not so loud as those that cry for hire. (***Emerson:** *The chief mourner does not always attend the funeral.)*

Hugo: *Great grief is a divine and terrible radiance which transfigures the wretched.*

Shakespeare: *...excessive grief the enemy to the living.*

Johnson: *Grief aids disease; remembered folly stings.*

Blake: *The busy bee has no time for sorrow. (***Young:** *Sorrow's best antidote is employment.)*

MAN'S PLACE IN THE UNIVERSE

Lucian: *We're all made of the same dust.* (**Babylonian Talmud, 450:** *You all spit the same spittle.*)

Chalmers: *The thousands that pass off the stage of life are no more remembered than yesterday's insects....Live for something.*

Emerson: *Those who live for the future must always seem selfish to those who live for the present.*

Homer: *As leaves on trees, such is the life of man/ Himself a shadow, hunting shadows.* (**Burke:** *What shadows we are, and what shadows we pursue.* **Wordsworth:** *We all laugh at pursuing a shadow, though the lives of the multitudes are devoted to the chase.*)

Sophocles: *We are all but phantoms, unsubstantial shadows.* (**I Chronicles, 300 BC:** *Our days on earth are as a shadow.* **Horace:** *We are but dust and shadow.*)

Petronius: *How we puffed-up bladders strut about....We are nothing but bubbles.*

Tennyson: *What is it all but a trouble of ants in the gleam/ of a million millions of suns? What but a murmur of gnats in the gloam, or a/ moment's anger of bees in their hives?*
  It is inconceivable that the whole Universe was merely created for us who live in this third-rate planet of a third-rate sun. (**Dixon:** *...inheriting for a moment the wrinkled surface of a burnt-out-star.*)

H.K. White: *What art thou in the scale of the universe?/ Less, less than nothing!*

Lowell: *Where we poor puppets, jerked by unseen wires....* (**Unknown:** *Men are puppets in the hands of God.*)

Plato: *The gods made men for their sport.* (**Dixon:** *The gods may be interested to see what we can make of the world....we are here by His will and inscrutable purpose....*)

Meredith: *We are but the instruments of heaven; our work is not design, but destiny.*
  Fate is not the ruler, but the servant of Providence.

Byron: *Men are the sport of circumstances, when/ The circumstances seem the sport of men.*

Balfour: *Nothing matters very much, and very few things matter at all.*

Tennyson: *Our little systems have their day.*

Dyer: *A little rule, a little sway,*
       A sunbeam in a winter's day,
       Is all the proud and mighty have
       Between the cradle and the grave.

Hubbard: *Man is Creation's masterpiece; but who says so? – Man.*

Browne: *...every man is a microcosm....*

Unknown: *God has delegated himself to a million deputies.*

Maugham: *...everything in the universe combines to cause every one of our actions....*

Aquinas: *Man has a destiny to which all his life and activities are directed.* (**Butler, 1680:** *We only row: we're steered by Fate.* **Herder:** *Man blindly works the will of fate.* **Firdusi:** *Man cannot strive with destiny.*)

Emerson: *Things work to their ends, not to yours....*

Lowell: *Chances have laws as fixed as planets have....*

Joubert: *Chance is a role that providence has reserved for itself in the affairs of the world so as to ensure that men would feel they have no influence.* (**I Corinthians 1:29** *That no flesh should glory in his presence.*)

Montaigne: *Heaven is jealous of the extent that we attribute to the right of human prudence above its own.*

Ansari: *The world is not a place for enjoyment, but a place where humanity is on trial.* (**Unknown:** *Life is a testing-ground for the Hereafter.*)

Lamartine: *Let us enjoy the fugitive hour. Man has no harbor, time has no shore, it rushes on and carries us with it.*

Thoreau: *You might say of a Philosopher that he was in this world as a spectator [or observer].*
How can you walk on ground when you see through it?

Dryden: *But how can finite grasp Infinity?* (**Roethke:** *All finite things reveal infinitude.*)

Psalms 8:3 (250 BC) *When I consider thy heavens, the work of thy fingers, the moon and the stars....what is man; that thou art mindful of him?*

Job 37:14 (350 BC) *...stand still and consider the wondrous works of God.*

35:6-7 *If thou sinnest, what doest thou against him? If thou be righteous, what givest thou to him?*

TIME and SPACE

Dr. Fuller: *Time devours all things.*

Young: *Naught treads so silent as the foot of time.*

Lucretius: *...time by itself does not exist....* (**Emerson:** *Space and time are but forms of thought.*)

Lamb: *Nothing puzzles me more than time and space; and yet troubles me less, as I never think about them.*

Cowper: *I have just time to observe that time is short, and by the time I have made the observation, time is gone....*

Tupper: *How should the Infinite be understood in Time, when it stretcheth on ungrasped forever?*

Emerson: *What would be the use of immortality to a person who cannot use well a half hour?*

Holmes: *A moment's insight is sometimes worth a life's experience.*

Syrus: *A single hour often restores what many years have taken away.*

Tupper: *The sting of pain and the edge of pleasure are blunted by long expectation.*

LITTLE THINGS

Pope: *What mighty contests rise from trivial things!*

Emerson: *He that despises little things shall perish by little and little. Society lives to trifles, and when men die we do not mention them. Trifles is a very convertible word. Your trifles are my gods.*

Thoreau: *I find myself oftenest wise in little things and foolish in great ones.*

Smith: *Trifles make up the happiness or the misery of mortal life.*

Lowell: *A stray hair, by its continual irritation, may give more annoyance than a smart blow.*

Joubert: *All beings come from little, and little is needed for them to come to nothing.*

NONSENSE WITH TEETH

Jackson: *By showing us the absurdity of things, nonsense may help to keep us usefully sane.*

Anonymous: *A little nonsense now and then/ Is relished by the wisest men.*

Wycherley: *Rhyme often makes mystical nonsense with the critics for wit.*

Unknown: *Shakespeare used more quotations than any other man.*

Unknown: *All my best thoughts were stolen by the ancients!*

Unknown: *No poet should have to spout his own verses.*

Farquhar: *Says little, thinks less and does - nothing at all, faith!*

Cowper: *I wrote my last letter merely to inform you that I had nothing to say; in answer to which you have said nothing.*

G. Eliot: *There's some as thinks one thing: there's some as thinks another thing: but my opinion is different.*

Unknown: *Defoe says there were a hundred-thousand stout country-fellows in his time ready to fight to the death against popery, without knowing whether popery was a man or a horse.*

Benchley: *...was born in a thatched hut, or hutched thatch, in Normandy. Or hatched thutch.*

Hood: *Seemed washing his hands with invisible soap/ In imperceptible water.*

Swift: *If a lump of soot falls into the soup, and you cannot conveniently get it out, stir it well in, and it will give the soup a French taste.*

He had been eight years upon a project for extracting sunbeams out of cucumbers, which were to be put into phials hermetically sealed, and let out to warm the air in raw, inclement summers.

Thomson: *A little, round, fat, oily man of God.*

Holmes: *I have always considered my face as a convenience rather than an ornament.*

Thoreau: *One wise sentence is worth the State of Massachusetts.*

Anonymous (18th cent.): *Rags make paper*
Paper makes money
Money makes banks
Banks make loans
Loans make beggars
Beggars make rags

Traditional: *Miss Smarty*
Gave a Party:
Nobody came.
Her brother
Gave another –
Just the same.

SIMPLICITY

St. Jerome: *My reverence has always been for holy simplicity rather than a wordy vulgarity.*

Newton: *Truth is ever to be found in simplicity and not in multiplicity and confusion of things.*

da Vinci: *Simplicity is the ultimate sophistication.*

Bovée: *Partial culture runs to ornate; the extreme culture to simplicity.*

Phillips Brooks: *The man who has begun to live more seriously within, begins to live more simply without.*

Euripides: *Life is simple when one is sick.*

Unknown: *The canker of care seems to eat the life away.*

Thoreau: *What you call bareness and poverty is to me simplicity.*

John Gay: *Whoever heard a man of fortune in England talk of the necessaries of life?*

Belloc: *Poverty makes men appreciate reality.*

Cicero: *Plain living and high thinking.*

WORK

Hardy: *Work was given us as an antidote, not as a punishment.*

Antisthenes: *Work is the essential good and source of satisfaction.* **(Latin proverb**: *Labor itself is a pleasure.* **G. Herbert:** *Play not for gain but for sport.* **Bias:** *The occupation which gives a man most pleasure is making money.* **Beecher:** *Very few men acquire wealth in such a manner as to receive pleasure from it. As long as there is the enthusiasm of the chase they enjoy it.* **Balguy:** *When a man's desires are boundless, his labors are endless.)*

Galen: *Employment is Nature's physician.*

Browning: *A minute's success pays the failure of years.*

Cowper: *Absence of occupation is not rest,/ A mind quite vacant is a mind distressed.* **(Pope:** *Too much rest itself becomes a pain.)*

Latin proverb: *The gods sell us all things at the price of labor.* **(Howell:** *Pains is the price that God puts upon all things.)*

Cicero: *...it is weariness of all pursuits that creates weariness of life.*

Southey: *Wise lesson this for me, thou busy busy bee! What is the end of thy toil?*

Thoreau: *...a man may be very industrious, and not spend his time well.*

Themistocles: *...not thinking fit to become slaves for the sake of things that have no life or soul....*

Ellis: *...make machines the slaves, instead of the masters of men.*

Seneca: *It is for the superfluous things of life that men sweat.* **(Sterne:** *Men tire themselves in pursuit of rest.)*

Marquis: *He worked like hell in the country/ so he could live in the city, where he/ worked like hell so he could live in the country!*

Kipling: *More men are killed by overwork than the importance of the world justifies.*

Goldsmith: *Those that think must govern them that toil.*

Ecclesiastes 6:7 (250 BC) *All the labour of man is for his mouth, and yet the appetite is not filled.*
1:8 *All things are full of labour; man cannot utter it; the eye is not satisfied with seeing, nor the ear filled with hearing.*
5:11 *...what good is there to the owners thereof, saving the beholding of them with their eyes?*
5:19 *Every man also to whom God hath given riches and wealth, and hath given him powers to eat thereof, and to take his portion, and to rejoice in his labour; this is the gift of God.*
1:3 *What profit hath a man of all his labour which he taketh under the sun?*

Psalms 127:1 *Except the Lord build the house, they labour in vain that build it; except the Lord keep the city, the watchman waketh but in vain.*

KNOWLEDGE

Job 35:16 (350 BC) *He multiplieth words without knowledge.*

Bacon: *The first great judgment of God upon the ambition of man was the confusion of tongues.*

Montaigne: *Most of the causes of the world's troubles are grammatical.*

Seneca: *The study of wisdom has become the study of words.*
Speech is the index of the mind. Where the speech is corrupted, the mind is also.

Berkeley: *[We] pervert the use of speech...to protract and multiply disputes where there is no difference of opinion.*
...entreat the reader to sound his own thoughts, and not suffer himself to be imposed on by words.

Horne: *Among the sources of those innumerable calamities which from age to age have overwhelmed mankind, may be reckoned as one of the principal, the abuse of words.* (**Spencer:** *How often misused words generate misleading thoughts.*)

Bacon: *[Human nature is] prone to abstractions....Men create oppositions which are not....*

Hsiang-Kuo: *...uncertainty between right and wrong...shows that the distinctions between right and wrong are due to partiality of view, and that all things are really in agreement.*

Lowell: *Truth wears a different face to everybody.*

Dryden: *For truth has such a face and such a mien/ As to be lov'd needs only to be seen.*

Daniel 12:4 (170 BC) *Many shall run to and fro, and knowledge shall be increased. [Information overload?]*

Maeterlinck: *All our knowledge merely helps us to die a more painful death than the animals who know nothing.*

Montaigne: *Nothing is so firmly believed as what is least known.*

Tacitus: *It is more religious and more reverent to believe in the works of the Deity than to comprehend them.*

Ecclesiasticus (190 BC) *Be not curious in unnecessary matters.* **(Ovid:** *It is well for man to be in ignorance of many things.)*

Pliny the Elder: *To inquire what is beyond it is no concern of man; nor can the human mind form any conjecture concerning it.*

Xenophon: *[Socrates] believed that any attempt to search out what the gods had not chosen to reveal must be displeasing to them....he who meddles with these matters runs the risk of losing his sanity.* **(Chas Churchill:** *With curious art the brain, too finely wrought,/ Preys on herself, and is destroyed by thought.)*

Dr. Fuller: *A thread too fine spun will easily break.*

Pascal: *...it is not so bad to be in error as to be curious to no purpose.*

Kempis: *There are many things, the knowledge of which is of little or no profit to the soul....such questions often beget useless strifes and contentions....*

Prior: *In argument similes are like songs in love;/ they describe much, but prove nothing.*

Thoreau: *The question is not what you look at but what you see.*

Whipple: *Sight must be reinforced by insight. [***Plato's*** contention that there is no final truth in sense perception.]*

Chas Churchill: *That evil is half-cured whose cause we know.*

Cicero: *The causes of events are always more interesting than the events themselves.*
  I would I could as easily discover the true as I can expose the false.

Holmes: *Genius is the capacity to reach the proper conclusion before all the facts are in.*

Vauvenargues: *Originality is the supreme evidence of genius.*

EDUCATION

Dumas: *How is it that although little children are so intelligent, most adults are so stupid? Education must have something to do with it.*

Wiggam: *Intelligence appears to be the thing that enables a man to get along without education, Education appears to be the thing that enables a man to get along without the use of intelligence.*

Keynes: *Education: the inculcation of the incomprehensible into the indifferent by the incompetent.*

Trevelyan: *Education has produced a vast population able to read, but unable to distinguish what is worth reading.*

Rousseau: *...all that sorry nonsense...that goes by the name of education.*

Hubbard: *...education is one thing and life another.* (**Robertson:** *Instruction ends in the classroom, but education ends only with life.*)

Bacon: *Universities incline wits to sophistry and affectation.*

Butler (1680): *Learned nonsense has a deeper sound,/ Than easy sense, and goes for more profound.*

Molière: *People of quality know everything without ever having been taught.*

Thoreau: *The scholar rarely writes as well as the farmer talks....How vain it is to sit down to write when you have not stood up to live!*
 I have now a library of nearly nine hundred volumes, over seven hundred of which I wrote myself.
 There are nowadays professors of philosophy, but not philosophers.

Blake: *The cistern contains: the fountain overflows.*

Kingsley: *...do not darken your mind with intellectual puzzles....*

H. Adams: *...philosophy, which consists chiefly in suggesting unintelligible answers to insoluble problems....*

Santayana: *Psychology attempts what is perhaps impossible, namely the anatomy of life.*

Emerson: *Colleges hate geniuses, just as convents hate saints.*

Milton: *Deep versed in books and shallow in himself.*
Where there is much desire to learn, there of necessity will be much arguing, much writing, many opinions....

Rogers: *When a new book appears read an old one.*

Callimachus: *Big book, big bore.*

Bacon: *Books can never teach the use of books.*

Spanish proverb: *Books and friends should be few and good.*
*(***Martial:** *It is my delight to give pleasure to a select few.)*

Holmes: *Systems die, instincts remain.*

Cowper: *Knowledge dwells/ In heads replete with thoughts of other men,/Wisdom in minds attentive to their own.*
...pedantry is all that schools impart.
How much a dunce that has been sent to roam/ Excels a dunce that has been kept at home.

Lao Tzu: *The further one travels [studies] the less one may know.*

Kempis: *What canst thou see abroad which thou seest not at home?*

Emerson: *The stuff of all countries is just the same. (***Unknown:** *Why should I travel when I am already here?)*

Tupper: *Memory is not wisdom; idiots can rote volumes: Yet, what is wisdom without memory?*

WORDS

Joubert: *The word, in fact, is disembodied thought.*

W. Churchill: *...art of arranging the right words in their proper order.*

Pascal: *Words differently arranged have a different meaning, and meanings differently arranged have different effects.*

Euripides: *...the force of words/ can do what is done by conquering swords.*

Whipple: *Felicity, not fluency of language, is a merit.*

Cato the Elder: *Speech is bestowed on all, sound sense on few.*

Plutarch: *Phocion expressed the most sense in the fewest words.*
(Pliny the Younger: *Nothing pleases so much as brevity.)*

Isaac D'Israeli: *With words we govern men.*

SELF-KNOWLEDGE

Hume: *The self is nothing but a collection of thoughts and experiences.*

Thales: *What is most difficult to man? To know oneself.*

Seneca: *It takes the whole of life to learn how to live. (***Bruyère:** *Man does not live long enough to profit from his faults.)*

Shakespeare: *Men's faults do seldom to themselves appear.*

Spurgeon: *Humility is to make a right estimate of oneself.*

Oldham: *And all your fortune lies beneath your hat.*

Xenophanes: *The key to understanding the nature of the world is* <u>introspection</u>: *'I went looking for myself.'*

Zimmerman: *...self-distrust is the first proof we give of having obtained a knowledge of ourselves.*

St. Bernard: *Many men are wise about many things, and ignorant about themselves.*

W. Churchill: *The power of man has grown in every sphere except over himself.*

Valéry: *Knowing oneself does not necessarily imply improving oneself.*

Moody: *I've had more trouble with myself than with any man I've ever met.*

Proverbs 20:24 (350 BC) *Man's goings are of the Lord; how can a man then understand his own way?*

Seneca: *If you would escape your troubles, you need not another place but another personality.*

Buck: *[Equanimity] is not dejected in adversity, nor elated in prosperity.*

Firkins: *My state is contentment within despair.*

Hazlitt: *To great evils we submit, we resent little provocations.*

Sophocles: *The evils we bring on ourselves are the hardest to bear.*

Emerson: *Every ship is a romantic object, except that we sail in.*
   The sea is lovely, but when we bathe in it, the beauty forsakes all the near water. For the imagination and senses cannot be gratified at the same time.

Beecher: *Age and youth look upon life from the opposite ends of the telescope.*

CHARACTER

Thoreau: *Manners are conscious; character is unconscious.*

Dr. Fuller: *Men are not to be measured by inches.*

Wycherley: *I weigh the man, not his title.*

Powers: *The eye is the window of the soul....The animals look for man's intentions right into his eyes.*

Ecclesiasticus (190 BC) *The heart of a man changeth his countenance, whether for good or for evil.*

Channing: *The inward moulds the outward.*

Unknown: *A greater sculptor than Michelangelo is Thought. What a man thinks in his heart he advertises with his face.*

Unknown: *What you are thinking shows through.*

Lincoln: *Every man over forty is responsible for his face.*

Ovid: *A man's habitual pursuits pass over into character.*

Plutarch: *Character is habit long continued.*

Dhammapada: *All that we are is the result of what we have thought.*

Chamfort: *A man of intellect is lost unless he unites it to energy of character.*

St. Matthew 12:34 *...out of the abundance of the heart the mouth speaketh.*

Saadi: *A jar exudes whatever it contains.*

Dr. Fuller: *When the heart is afire, some sparks will fly out of the mouth.*

Hazlitt: *Gracefulness has been defined to be the outward expression of the inward harmony of the soul.*

Riccoboni: *Fortune does not change men; it only unmasks them.*

Cowper: *Faults in the life breed errors in the brain,/ And these, reciprocally, those again.*

Prior: *Every man is mad on some point.*

Bruyère: *...the self-satisfied man produces the self-important man.*

Browning: *As if true pride/ Were not also humble!*

MIND

Anaxagoras: *And mind, which is eternal....infinite....over all is mind the ruler.*

Ignatius: *Even the things you do after the flesh are spiritual.*

Bacon: *The mind is the man.* (**Proverb:** *What's a man but his mind?*)

Emerson: *The key to every man is his thought....What is life but what a man is thinking of all day?*
  Minds are lenses of different convexity....Some men see microscopically: some see telescopically. One magnifies, and one microfies.

W. Motherwell: *...the reciprocal influence of mind and body!*

Tupper: *Worms may batten on the brain; but can worms gnaw the mind?*

Thoreau: *...original thinking is the divinest thing.*

Carlyle: *Metaphysics is the attempt of the mind to rise above the mind....Hopeless struggle....[Can a man] lift up himself?* (**T.S. Eliot:** *...to draw a sharp line between metaphysics and common sense would itself be metaphysics and not common sense.*)

Mencken: *The human mind...cannot grasp the concept of nothingness....*

Chesterton: *If everything changes, including mind of man, how can we tell whether any change is an improvement or no?*

Cicero: *The bond of society is reason and speech. In nothing [than by reason] are we further removed from the nature of wild beasts.* (**Sandburg:** *So long as we speak the same language and never understand each other.*)

Trench: *Language is the amber in which a thousand precious thoughts have been safely embedded and preserved.* (**Bovée:** *Books are embalmed minds.* **Longfellow:** *Books are sepulchres of thought.*)

Latin proverb: *Life without literature is death.*

Spencer: *Reading is seeing by proxy.*

Pythagoras: *A thought is an idea in transit.*

Jackson: *Ideas are not the product of thought; they are flashes of light from the unknown. Deliberation is barren.*

Milton: *Thou canst not touch the freedom of my mind.*

S.T. Coleridge: *If you are not a thinking man, to what purpose are you a man at all?*

Thoreau: *He is a rich man...who can feel delight in his own thoughts.* (**Milton:** *Think only what concerns thee and thy being.*)
   If I am visited by a thought, I chew that cud...as long as there is any flavor in it until my keepers shake down some fresh fodder.
Bacon: *Thoughts that come unsought for are commonly the most valuable....* (**Tacitus:** *These things are more pleasing which spring of their own accord.* **Seneca:** *Nothing can be so profitable as to be so when negligently read.*)

Molière: *I take back my property wherever I find it.* (**Emerson:** *Thought is the property of him who can entertain it.*)

Vauvenargues: *[All] Great thoughts come from the heart.* (**Lowell:** *All thought begins in feeling.*)

S.T. Coleridge: *What comes from the heart goes to the heart.* (**Sandburg:** *There is a touch of two hands that foils all dictionaries.*)
Wilcox: *Flesh thrills to thrilling flesh,/ Mind answers unto mind.*
Campbell: *Oh, hard it is to find/ The one just suited to our mind!*

Cowper: ...*we think as we are made to think....Thus am I both free and a prisoner at the same time. [Ditto for free will!]*

Cicero: *Dotage is not characteristic of all old men but only of the light-minded.* (**Johnson:** *It is a man's own fault, it is from want of use, if his mind grows torpid in old age.*)

Bryant: *Old age is wise for itself, but not for the community.*

Meredith: *A mind once cultivated will not lie fallow for half an hour.* (**Bovée**: *Mind unemployed is mind unenjoyed.*)

Wordsworth: *Their inward eye/ Which is the bliss of solitude.* (**Blake:** *And leads you to believe a lie/ When you see with, not through, the eye.*)

Thoreau: *You cannot see anything until you are clear of it.* (**Glanvill:** *The beauty of truth, as of a picture, is not acknowledged but at a distance.*)

Fontenelle: *We seem to recognize a truth the first time we hear it.* **Smith:** *A man gazing at the stars is proverbially at the mercy of the puddles on the road.*

Proverbs 20:12 (350 BC) *The hearing ear and the seeing eye; the Lord hath made even both of them.*

16:22 *Understanding is a wellspring of life unto him that hath it.* (**Stoic maxim, 300 BC** *The wise man alone is free, and every fool is a slave.*)

Babylonian Talmud (450) *He who is loud in his prayers is short in his faith. The reward of study is understanding.*

Cowper: *...a very robust athletic habit seems inconsistent with much sensibility.*

Plato: *I have hardly ever known a mathematician who was capable of reasoning.* (**Pascal:** *...it is rare that mathematicians are intuitive...and that men of intuition are mathematicians.*)

WISDOM

Unknown: *The greatest challenge in life is to decide what is important and disregard everything else.*

Rochefoucauld: *The greatest of all gifts is the power to estimate things at their true worth.* **(Bruyère:** *The remedy for [being overcome by petty sorrows] is to value the things of the world at no more than their true worth.)*

Southey: *Philosophy teaches us to value all things at their real worth, to be contented with little, modest in prosperity, patient in trouble, equal-minded at all times.*

Dean Inge: *By wisdom I mean a just estimate of the relative values of things.* **(H. More:** *It is not so important to know everything as to know the exact value.)*

Molière: *Esteem is based on some preference: to esteem all is to esteem no one.*

Osler: *The value of experience is not in seeing much, but in seeing wisely.*

Colton: *I have always considered rather what is said than who says it....*

Zangwill: *What is a cynic? An accurate observer of life!*

S.T. Coleridge: *To most men, experience is like the stern lights of a ship, which illuminates only the track it has passed.* **(Roux:** *Our experience is composed rather of illusions lost than of wisdom acquired.)*

Johnson: *Wisdom calms the mind.*

Emerson: *Wisdom is insight....Wisdom is like electricity...as glasses rubbed aquire electric power for a while....There is no permanent wise man....*

Euripides: *Humility/ And respect for the gods is the only wisdom.*

Ruskin: *Great men have a feeling that the greatness is not in them, but through them.*

Bruyère: *...where wisdom is lacking, find greatness if you can.*

Hippocrates: *Things that are holy are revealed only to men who are holy.* (**Euripides:** *Wisdom to the unwise means nothing.* **Lezinsky:** *Genius speaks only to genius.)*

HAPPINESS

Euripides: *...no man among mortals is happy:/ If wealth comes to a man, he may be luckier/ Than the rest; but happy - never.*

*The childless, through ignorance of them,/ Have never discovered if children/ Will be a delight or a sorrow/ To men, and avoid much grief. (**Bacon:** He that hath wife and children hath given hostages to fortune....)*

Man's best possession is a sympathetic wife.

Hubbard: *Health and happiness can be found only out of doors.*

Orwell: *Men can only be happy when they do not assume that the object of life is happiness. (**Jackson:** Those who are careless of happiness are happy.)*

Meredith: *We lose the peace of years when we hunt after the rapture of moments.*

Hazlitt, paraphrasing Hume: *...all satisfactions are equal, because the cup can be no more than full.*

Tolstoy: *...the eternal error men make in imagining that happiness is the realization of their desires....*

St. Augustine: *Happiness consists in having only right desires.*

Socrates: *Having the fewest wants, I am nearest to the gods. How many things I can do without!*

Rochefoucauld: *He is happiest whom very little contents. (**Einstein:** I am happy because I want nothing from anyone.)*

Johnson: *Where necessity ends, desire and curiosity begin; no sooner are we supplied with everything nature can demand, then we sit down to contrive artificial appetites.*

Thoreau: *How many a man has dated a new era in his life from the reading of a book.*

Cicero: *There can be no greater pleasures than those of the mind. To live is to think.* (**Gilbert:** *Philosophy is for the few.*)

Phelps: *The happiest person is the person who thinks the most interesting thoughts, and we grow happier as we grow older.*

Humboldt: *Insight into universal nature provides an intellectual delight and sense of freedom that no blows of fate and no evil can destroy.*

Wolff: *...reason is nothing other than the insight into the connection between truths.*

Seneca: *There is no tranquillity but that which reason confers. Life is more delightful when it is on the downward slope.*

Santayana: *Animals are born and bred in litters. Solitude grows blessed and peaceful only in old age.*

Voltaire: *The happiest of all lives is a busy solitude.*

Moore: *The heaven of each is but what each desires.*

Leigh Hunt: *A fireside is a great opiate.*

Marlowe: *Infinite riches in a little room.*

Dr. Fuller: *It is comparison that makes men happy or miserable.*

Bacon: *...where there is no comparison, no envy.... [Comparisons are always invidious.]*

Hugo: *Melancholy is the pleasure of being sad.*

MUSIC

Thos. Fuller: *Music is nothing else but wild sounds civilised into time and tune.* (**Thoreau:** *Music is the crystallization of sound.*)

Tupper: *Wherefore is the ear attuned to a pleasure in musical sounds,/ And who set a number to those sounds, and fixed the laws of harmony?*

Thoreau: *The strains of the aeolian harp and of the wood thrush are the truest and loftiest preachers that I know now left on this earth.*
...so few habitually intoxicate themselves with music, so many with alcohol.

Richter: *Music is too good for drinking-songs and merry-makings.*

Milton: *Such sweet compulsion doth in music lie.*

Congreve: *Music hath charms to soothe a savage breast.*

Dryden: *What passion cannot music raise and quell?*

Shelley: *Our sweetest songs are those that tell of saddest thought.* (*'Sad Songs Mean So Much'*)

Wordsworth: *Sweetest melodies/ Are those that are by distance made more sweet.*

Beethoven: *Music is a higher revelation than theology.*

Nietzsche: *Without music life would be a mistake.*

FRIENDSHIP

Santayana: *Everyone has had a father and a mother; but how many have had a friend?*

Cartwright: *There are two births: the one when light/ First strikes the new awaken'd sense;/ The other when two souls unite....*

Jackson: *Friendship is mutual curiosity.*

Thoreau: *To attain a true relation to one human creature is enough to make a year memorable.*
   What is the singing of birds, or any natural sound, compared with the one we love?
   ...no exertion of the legs can bring two minds much nearer to one another.

Emerson: *Two human beings are like globes, which can touch only in a point.*
   Every man alone is sincere. At the entrance of a second person, hypocrisy begins.
   'Do you love me?' means at last, 'Do you see the same truth I see?'

Jackson: *A man's spiritual kin are his nearest relations.*

Smith: *...love is but the discovery of ourselves in others, and the delight in the recognition.*

THE SEXES

Rowland: *Life is a game in four rubbers: hearts are trumps when a man is young; clubs are trumps as he waxes rich and gouty; and lastly - spades.*

No matter how much a man dislikes children before marriage, after marriage he always imagines that he is going to improve on the human race.

Johnson: *One cannot love lumps of flesh, and little infants are nothing more.*

Pope: *They dream in courtship, but in wedlock wake.*

Rogers: *It does not much signify whom one marries, as one is sure to find next morning that it is someone else.*

John Gay: *Do you think your mother and I should have lived comfortably so long together if ever we had been married?*

Johnson: *Wise married women don't trouble themselves about infidelity in their husbands....*

S.T. Coleridge: *Marriage has no <u>natural</u> relation to love. Marriage belongs to society; it is a social contract.*

Jackson: *Man has to be seduced into reproducing his kind. But in the sterilisation of marriage he takes his revenge.*

Emerson: *Most men and women are merely one couple more. Thus most men are mere bulls and most women cows....*

Lawrence: *[Men] are all dogs that trot and sniff and copulate.*

Wordsworth: *Maidens withering on the stalk.*

Molière: *A woman is like ivy, which grows beautifully as long as it twines about a tree, but is of no use when it is separated.*

Leigh Hunt: *The two divinest things this world has got,/ A lovely woman in a rural spot.*

Madame Fée: *...there is nothing more incompatible with women's natural vocation than rivalry with men.*

Johnson: *Nature has given woman so much power that the law cannot afford to give her more.*

Staël: *Love is the very history of a woman's life; it is merely an episode in a man's.*

Edwards: *If a man understands one woman he should let it go at that.*

Saadi: *A sweet voice is better than a beautiful face. (***Greene:** *Rather love by the ear than like by the eye.)*

Farquhar: *Charming women can true converts make,/ We love the precepts for the teacher's sake.*

Moore: *The light that lies/ In woman's eyes,/ Has been my heart's undoing.*

Young: *...gazed with such intensity of love, sending his soul out to me in a look.*

H. Coleridge: *Her loveliness I never knew/ Until she smiled on me./ Oh! then I saw her eye was bright,/ A well of love, a spring of light.*

Stevenson: *What sound is so full of music as one's own name uttered for the first time in the voice of her we love!*

Thomson: *Loveliness is when unadorned, adorned the most.*

Waller: *The yielding marble of her snowy breast.*

Blackmore: *...the dark soft weeping of her hair, and the shadow light of her eyes (like a wood rayed through with sunset)....*

Tennyson: *Roses are her cheeks,/ And a rose her mouth.*

Johnson: *Kindness is in our power: but fondness is not.*

Dobson: *Love comes unseen; we only see it go.*

Thoreau: *Love is a thirst that is never slaked.*

Campbell: *Love's wing moults when caged and captured....* (**Byron:** *Friendship is Love without his wings.*)

Proverb: *Kissin' don't last, good cookin' do.*

Proverb: *Sudden love lasts longest.*

Molière: *The whole pleasure in love lies in the variety.* (**Prior:** *Variety alone gives joy./ The sweetest meats the soonest cloy.*)

Farquhar: *The shortest pleasures are the sweetest.* (**Leigh Hunt:** *Stolen kisses are always sweetest.*)

Byron: *All farewells should be sudden.*

Landon: *Were it not better to forget/ Than but remember and regret?*

Italian proverb: *Below the navel there is neither religion nor truth.*

Pope: *'Old fish at table, but young flesh in bed.'*
  Beauty draws us with a single hair.

Joubert, on the sexes: *One has the look of a wound, the other of something skinned.*

Colton: *...the body too often lords it over the mind.*

Johnson: *Were it not for imagination, a man would be as happy in the arms of a chambermaid as a duchess.*

Edwards: *Without clothes there would be no nudity.*

Thoreau: *I lose my respect for the man who can make the mystery of sex the subject of a coarse jest....*

Juvenal: *Young men differ in various ways, but old men all look alike.*

Dillon: *Old men are only walking hospitals.*

CUSTOM, CONFORMITY

Seneca: *We live not according to reason, but according to fashion.*

Emerson: *We live for purposes of exhibition chiefly....We pain ourselves to please nobody....Our expense is almost all for conformity.*
  Society is a masked ball, where everyone hides his real character, and reveals it by hiding.
  A man no longer conducts his own life. It is manufactured for him.

Thoreau: *Be not simply obedient like the vegetables.*
  If I am not I, who will be?

Plutarch: *...the desire of riches does not proceed from a natural passion within us, but arises rather from vulgar out-of-doors opinion of other people.*

Wordsworth: *Habit rules the unreflecting herd.* (**Scott:** *One sheep will leap the ditch when another goes first.*)
  The dreary intercourse of daily life. (**Thoreau:** *We meet at meals three times a day, and give each other a new taste of that old musty cheese that we are.*)

Mencken: *[Civilization] under democracy tends to degenerate into a mere combat of crazes.*

Johnson: *I found that generally what was new was false.*

Stevenson: *Man is a creature who lives...principally by catchwords....*

Euripides: *And you only think you are thinking.*

Cobbett: *Free yourself from the slavery of tea and coffee and other slopkettle.*

Young: *Born originals, how comes it to pass that we die copies?*

S.T. Coleridge: *How inimitably graceful children are before they learn to dance!*

Voltaire: *Very few are able to raise themselves above the ideas of their times.*

Santayana: *Nothing is more treacherous than tradition; when insight and force are lacking to keep it warm.*

Ballou: *...tradition is apt to repeat it [falsehood] for truth.*

Saint Cyprian: *Custom is often only the antiquity of error.* **(G. Herbert:** *Custom without reason is but ancient error.)*

Plutarch: *We are more sensible of what is done against custom than against Nature.*

Bacon: *...lay aside received opinions and notions....*

Marquis: *Nothing changes all the bunk/ of long ago/ progress always stubs its toe*

Comte: *The dead govern the living.*

Howe: *The way of this world is to praise dead saints and persecute living ones.*

Montesquieu: *There is no more cruel tyranny than that which is exercised under the cover of law.*

Thomson: *It is success that colors all in life.*

Wycherley: *Poets, like whores, are only hated by each other.*

H. More: *In men this blunder still you find,/ All think their little set mankind.*

Simms: *The proverb answers where the sermon fails.* **(Anonymous:** *Proverbs are the cream of a nation's thought.)*

FOLLY

French proverb: *Evil is whatever does harm.*

Shakespeare: *The common curse of mankind - folly and ignorance. What men daily do, not knowing what they do!*

Goldsmith: *Nothing can exceed the vanity of our existence but the folly of our pursuits....To pursue trifles is the lot of humanity.*

Wiggam: *Many who multiply the most have not sufficient intelligence to add.*

Latin proverb: *We torture ourselves miserably over trifles.*

Philolaus: *He lamented, too, the futility of the lives most men live, not seeking enduring wisdom.*

Thoreau: *The mass never comes up to the standard of its best member, but on the contrary degrades itself to a level with the lowest.*
...the mind can be permanently profaned by the habit of attending to trivial things....
It is surprising what a tissue of trifles and crudities make the daily news.

Prior: *What trifling coil do we poor mortals keep;/ Wake, eat and drink, evacuate and sleep.*

Pope: *Fix'd like a plant in his peculiar spot,/ To draw nutrition, propagate and rot.* (**Lowell:** *The unmotivated herd that only feed and sleep.*)

Voltaire: *It is with books as with men: a very small number play a great part, the rest are lost in the multitude.*

Plautus: *How great in number are the little-minded men.*

Butler (1680): *There are more fools than knaves in the world,/ else the knaves would not have enough to live upon.*

Emerson: *...if a man sits down to think, he is immediately asked if he has the headache.*

Joubert: *We live in an age in which superfluous ideas abound and essential ideas are lacking.*

Walpole: *...this world is a comedy to those that think, a tragedy to those that feel - a solution of why Democritus laughed and Heraclitus wept.*

Bruyère: *Most men spend the best part of their lives making the remaining part miserable.*
 He is unaware of birth, he suffers at death, and he forgets to live.

Clarendon: *...who have lived to no purpose; who have rather breathed than lived.*

Ballou: *Real happiness is cheap enough, yet how dearly we pay for its counterfeit.*

Goldsmith: *...their chief and constant care/ Is to seem everything but what they are.*

Pliny the Younger: *Careless of things which are near, we pursue eagerly things which are far away.*

Thoreau: *The man who is often thinking it is better to be somewhere else than where he is excommunicates himself.*

Franklin: *Pain wastes the body, pleasures the understanding.*

Garin: *Many a fool feeds on pleasure. (****Young:** *Most pleasures, like flowers, when gathered, die.)*

Plutarch: *...vulgar display and luxury, the mistaken happiness of people that know no better thing than pleasure and self-indulgence.*

Shakespeare: *All things that are/ Are with more spirit chased than enjoyed.*

Goldsmith: *And the loud laugh that spoke the vacant mind.*

Pope: *Eternal smiles his emptiness betray,/ As shallow streams run dimpling all the way.*
  Amusement is the happiness of those who cannot think.

Chapin: *Gayety is often the reckless ripple over depths of despair.*

Southey: *All are not merry that seem mirthful.* (**Marquis:** *The saddest ones are those that wear/ The jester's motley garb.*)

Wordsworth: *As high as we have mounted in delight,/ In our dejection do we sink as low.*

Ellis: *The place where optimism most flourishes is the lunatic asylum.*

Fontaine: *We attribute our successes to our own sagacity, our failures to fortune.*

Molière: *We can commit every imaginable crime...and then excuse ourselves on the grounds that our destiny impelled us to do so.*

Milton: *The rabble praise and they admire/ they know not what, and know not whom,/ but as one leads the other.*
  License they mean when they cry Liberty!

Cowper: *He finds his fellow guilty of a skin/ Not coloured like his own.*

F. Amiel: *The era of equality means the triumph of mediocrity.*

Southey: *Popularity, a splash in the great pool of oblivion.*

Wordsworth: *Minds that have nothing to confer/ Find little to perceive. A primrose by a river's Brim/ A yellow primrose was to him,/ And it was nothing more.*

Tupper: *Few men, drinking at a rivulet, stop to consider its source.*

Rochefoucauld: *Truth does less good in the world than its appearances do harm.*

Epictetus: *Men are disturbed not by things, but by the views which they take of things.* (**Aurelius:** *It is our false opinions of things which ruin us.*)

Berkeley: *Few men think, yet all have opinions....the unreflecting (which are the far greater) part of mankind.*

Fontaine: *Contact with the world either breaks or hardens the heart.*

Behn: *He that will live in this world must be endowed with the three rare qualities of dissimulation, equivocation, and mental reservation.*

Bismarck: *There is nothing on this earth but hypocrisy, and jugglery....*

Blake: *General good is the plea of the scoundrel, hypocrite, and flatterer. Prisons are built with stones of law,/ brothels with bricks of religion.*

Goldsmith: *Lawyers are always more ready to get a man into troubles than out of them.*

Butler (1680): *Oaths are but words, and words but wind.*

Hesiod: *...trust and mistrust alike ruin man.*

Shakespeare: *They are as sick that surfeit with too much/ as they that starve with nothing.*
   You pay a great deal too dear for what's given freely.

Seneca: *It is for the superfluous things of life that men sweat....*

Cowper: *A life of ease a difficult pursuit.* (**Dixon:** *Your easy chair is your great breeder of melancholia....*)

Bradley: *Self-sacrifice is too often the 'great sacrifice' of trade, the giving cheap what is worth nothing.*

Ritson: *With wealth that he by roguery got/ Eight almshouses he built.*

Emerson: *Take egotism out, and you would castrate the benefactors....*
   Philanthropies and charities have a certain air of quackery.

Cowper: *Doing good/ Disinterested good, is not our trade.*

Massinger: *He that does public good for multitudes, finds few are truly grateful.*

WAR, POWER

Louis Napoleon: *War is but organized barbarism.*

Jerrold: *...what is war, nine times out of ten, but murder in uniform?*

Young: *One to destroy, is murder by the law;/ to murder thousands, takes a specious name,/ War's glorious art, and gives immortal fame.*

Gray: *The paths of glory lead but to the grave.*

Ficke: *Old men in impotence can beget/ New wars to kill the lusty young.*

Hubbard: *A soldier is a slave....His head is a superfluity. He is only a stick used by men to strike other men.*

Italian proverb: *The people murder one another, and princes embrace one another.* (**Congreve:** *War is the sport of kings.*)

Porteous: *Princes were privileged to kill, and numbers sanctified the crime.*

Campbell: *What millions died - that Caesar might be great!*

Pope: *Party-spirit, which at best is but the madness of many for the gain of the few.*

Bruyére: *In all ages men, for the sake of some small patch of ground, have...from one century to the next...been improving their methods of mutual destruction.*

Plautus: *Men prey on one another.*

Southey: *Now tell us all about the war,/ And what they fought each other for.*

Sandburg: *Liberty, Equality, Fraternity - I asked/ Why men die for words.*

   And the stonecutters earn a living - with lies - / on the tombs of the liars.

Montaigne: *[Men] stake their blood and their lives in quarrels wherein they have no manner of concern.*

Tacitus: *They create desolation and call it peace.* (**Milton:** *Wasting the earth, each other to destroy.*)

Scott: *...when men are freed from fighting for necessity, they quarrel through ambition.*

Milton: *Who overcomes/ By force hath overcome but half his foe.*

Corneille: *Who holds all power must fear everything.*

   The worst of all states is the people's state. (**Plato:** *Democracy passes into despotism.*)

Bacon: *It is a strange desire to seek power and to lose liberty, or to seek power over others and to lose power over a man's self.*

Mencken: *The urge to save humanity is almost always only a false-face for the urge to rule it. Power is what all messiahs really seek: not the chance to serve....We all play parts when we face our fellow-men....Man always seeks to rationalize his necessities....*

Maupassant: *Patriotism is a kind of religion; it is the egg from which wars are hatched.*

Dryden: *A mob is the scum that rises upmost when the nation boils.*

Latin proverb: *Where it is well with me, there is my country.* (**Milton:** *Where liberty dwells, there is my country.*)

MATERIALISM

Emerson: *Things are in the saddle,/ And ride mankind.*

Dean Inge: *They are idealists in their devotions and in their philosophy, but materialists in their charities and politics.*

Petronius: *What use are laws where money alone holds sway?*

Bion: *Money is the sinews of business.* (**Libanius:** *Money is the sinews of war.*)

Pope: *There should be as little merit in loving a woman for her beauty, as a man for his prosperity, both being equally subject to change.*

Emerson: *They measure their esteem of each other by what each has, and not by what each is.*

St. Luke 12:15 *...a man's life consisteth not in the abundance of the things which he possesseth.* (**Unknown:** *The real measure of our wealth is how much we should be worth if we lost our money..* **B.C. Forbes:** *Riches are mental, not material.*)

Wordsworth: *To think that now our life is only drest/ For show..../ The wealthiest man among us is the best..../ Plain living and high thinking are no more.*

Ruskin: *There is no wealth but life.* (**Johnson:** *It is better to live rich, than to die rich.*)

Proverbs 13:7 (350 BC) *There is that maketh himself rich, yet hath nothing: there is that maketh himself poor, yet hath great riches.* (**I Corinthians 6:10** *...having nothing, and yet possessing all things.*)

Words marking the grave of Nicos Kazantzakis on Crete: *I fear nothing. I hope for nothing. I am free.* (**Diderot:** *It's the philosopher who has nothing and asks for nothing.*)

Kipling, warning his audience against concern for money: *Some day you will meet a man who cares for none of these things. Then you will know how poor you are.*

Pliny the Younger: *An object in possession never retains the same charms it had in pursuit.* (**Gracián:** *Possession hinders enjoyment.*)

Thoreau: *Possessions are like leg-irons.* (**Maxwell:** *The more you own the more you are possessed.*)
I have found nothing so truly impoverishing as what is called wealth.

Seneca: *For many men, the acquisition of wealth does not end their troubles, it only changes them.*

Salomon Ibn Gabirol: *The end of wisdom is peace and tranquillity, whilst that of gold is grief and vexation.*

Saadi: *A beggar free from care is richer than a troubled king.* (**Shakespeare:** *I am sure care's an enemy to life.*)

Emerson: *Money often costs too much.* (**Stevenson:** *The price we pay for money is paid in liberty.*)

Penn: *Too few know when they have enough, and fewer know how to employ it.*

Goldsmith: *Ill fares the land, to hastening ills a prey,/ Where wealth accumulates, and men decay.*

Wordsworth: *Getting and spending, we lay waste our powers:/ Little we see in Nature that is ours.*

Marquis: *each generation wastes a little more/ of the future with greed and lust for riches.*
...he gives up/ everything else to get money/ and then discovers that it is not worth/ what he gave up to get it.

Proverbs 28:20 (350 BC) *Hell and destruction are never full; so the eyes of man are never satisfied.*

Davies: *Man lives to fret/ For some vain thing/ He cannot get.*

Arabic proverb: *Nothing but a handful of dust will fill the eye of man.*

Epitaph for Alexander the Great: *A tomb now suffices him for whom the whole world was not sufficient.*

Browne: *To me avarice seems not so much a vice, as a deplorable piece of madness.* (**Leigh Hunt:** *Building as if they were to live forever.*)

Psalms 106:15 (350 BC) *And he gave them their request; but sent leanness into their soul.* (**Unknown:** *Be careful what you wish for....* **Allan Updegraff:** *The fool's gold commonly called success.*)

Chesterton: *To be clever enough to get a great deal of money, one must be stupid enough to want it.*

Psalms 49:10 *The stupid and the senseless alike perish/ And leave their wealth to others.*

39:6 (250 BC) *He amasses riches and does not know who will gather them.*

62:10 *...if riches increase, set not your heart upon them.*

Franklin: *The use of money is all the advantage there is in having it.*

Emerson: *Money is of no value, it cannot spend itself. All depends on the skill of the spender.*

Lamb: *...the mercantile spirit levels all distinctions....Gain, and the pursuit of gain, sharpen a man's visage.*

Mann: *The pulpit teaches to be honest, the market-place trains to overreaching and fraud.*

Anacharsis: *The market place is a place set apart where men may deceive and overreach each other.*

Vauvenargues: *Commerce is the school of cheating.* (**Thoreau:** *...trade curses everything it handles....*)

Crabbe: *And the cold charities of man to man.*

Landon: *Few, save the poor, feel for the poor.*

G. Eliot: *One must be poor to know the luxury of giving.*

Surtees: *...having nothing a year, paid quarterly.*

SCIENCE

Rabelais: *Wisdom enters not into a malicious mind, and science without conscience is but the ruin of the soul.* (**G. Herbert:** *Knowledge is but folly, unless it is guided by grace.* **Einstein:** *Religion without science is blind. Science without religion is lame.*)

Proverb: *Much science, much sorrow.*

Pope*: Who shall decide when doctors disagree?*

Byron: *[Science is]/ But an exchange of ignorance for that/ Which is another kind of ignorance.*

Edwards: *All science, in fact, rests on a basis of faith, for it assumes the permanence and uniformity of natural laws - a thing which can never be demonstrated.*

Chesterton: *What much modern science fails to realise is that there is little use in knowing without thinking.*

Tolstoy: *What is called science today consists of a haphazard heap of information, united by nothing.*

Einstein: *Instead of freeing us...from spiritually exhausting labor, science has made men into slaves of machinery.* (**Unknown:** *A perfection of means and confusion of aims seems to be our main problem.*)

Emerson: *[In science] the end is lost sight of in attention to the means....*
  Chemistry takes to pieces, but it does not construct.
  After all our accumulation of facts we are just as poor in thought....
Not the fact avails but the use you make of it.
  The Idealist regards matter scientifically. The sensualist exclusively.

S.T. Coleridge: *Materialists unwilling to admit the mysterious element of our nature make it all mysterious.*

Spencer: *Life in its essence cannot be conceived in physico-chemical terms.* (**Wordsworth:** *We murder to dissect.*)

Sherrington: *The microscope merely resolves the mystery into some millions of separate microscopic growing points, each still a mystery....*

Dryden: *The sweetest essences are always confined in the smallest glasses.* (**Emerson:** *Physics carries centuries of observation in a single formula.*)

Hugo: *Where the telescope ends, the microscope begins. Which of the two has the grander view?*

Peacock: *...it is the ultimate destiny of science to exterminate the human race.* (**Emerson:** *The end of the human race will be that it will eventually die of civilization.*)

Hare: *The ultimate tendency of civilization is toward barbarism.*

Emerson: *Sir John Franklin went to find the NW passage and perished. The Esquimaux were there already, and are still thriving where he could not live.*

Thoreau: *The inhumanity of science concerns me....*

NATURE

Dante: *Nature is the art of God.*

Kingsley: *Study nature as the countenance of God.*

Emerson: *The world is mind precipitated....Spirit is matter reduced to an extreme thinness.*
  The whole world is a series of balanced antagonisms.

Cowper: *Nature is but a name for an effect*
          Whose cause is God.
          Not a flower
          But shows some touch in freckle,
          streak, or stain,
          of His unrivalled pencil.

Pope: *All Nature is but Art, unknown to thee;/ All Chance, Direction, which thou canst not see....*

Seneca: *What else is nature but God?* (**Proverb:** *Nature, the Handmaid of God Almighty.*)

Parker: *The lilies are redolent of God.*

Emerson: *He that made the world lets that speak for him, and does not employ a town crier.*
  We can never surprise nature in a corner, never find the end of a thread....
  Nature and books belong to the eyes that see them.. (**Thoreau:** *Beauty is where it is perceived.*
  The highest law gives a thing to him who can use it.)

Dixon: *Light, which makes all else visible, is itself invisible.*

Blake: *To see a world in a grain of sand*
And a heaven in a wild flower,
Hold infinity in the palm of your hand
And eternity in an hour.

Whitman: *After you have exhausted what there is in business, politics, conviviality, and so on - have found that none of these finally satisfy, or permanently wear - what remains? Nature remains.*

Thoreau: *The universe expects every man to do his duty in his parallel of latitude.*
My profession is to be always on the alert to find God in nature....

Bovée: *The loveliest faces are to be seen by moonlight, when one sees half with the eye, and half with the fancy.*
...the moon never appears so lustrous as when it emerges from a cloud.

De Quincey: *The laughter of girls is, and ever was, among the delightful sounds of earth.*

Thoreau: *The earth moves round the sun with inconceivable rapidity, and yet the surface of the lake is not ruffled by it.*
The earth is so bare that it makes an impression on me as if it were catching cold.
I think the heavens have had but one coat of paint since I was a boy, and their blue is pallid and dingy and worn off in many places....Me thinks the skies need a new coat. Have our eyes any blue to spare?
The most beautiful thing in nature is the sun reflected from a tearful cloud.
How pleasant the sound of water flowing with a hollow sound under ice from which it has settled away....Where the water gurgles under a natural bridge, you may hear [small cakes of ice] hold conversation in an undertone.

Smith: *In the wake of a ship there is always a melancholy splendour.*

Franklin: *And weeping willows bend to kiss the stream.*

Tennyson: *I heard the ripple washing in the reeds,/ And the wild water lapping on the crag.*
The myriad shriek of wheeling ocean-fowl,/ The league-long roller thundering on the reef.
The moan of doves in immemorial elms,/ And murmuring of innumerable bees.
A little street half garden and half house.

Goldsmith: *Sweet as the primrose peeps beneath the thorn.*

Keats: *And gathering swallows twitter in the skies.*

Ornithologist Alexander Wilson: *Bury me where the birds will sing over my grave.*

Roberts: *[Hermit thrush] fluting out his lonely and tranquil ecstasy.... a strain which, more than any other bird song on this earth, leaves the listener's heart aching exquisitely for its completion.*

Grayson: *...the old gray hen, a garrulous fowl, came and stood on one leg and looked at me first with one eye and then with the other.*

Thoreau: *We would keep hens, not for eggs, but to hear the cocks crow and the hens cackle.*
...the frogs were eructating...the bursting of mephitic air-bubbles rising from the bottom, a sort of blubbering....They suggest flatulency.

Mary Allen: *The little chickens, as they dip*
Their beaks into the river,
Hold up their heads at every sip,
And thank the Giver.

Billings: *Crows assemble in the fall of the year in annual conference... and appoint their deacons, elders, committees and advisory boards for the ensuing year.*

Emerson: *Foxes are so cunning/ Because they are not strong.*

Chris Smart, on cats: *For he is a mixture of gravity and waggery....For there is nothing sweeter than his peace at rest.*

H.S. Leigh: *My love she is a kitten,/ And my heart's a ball of string.*

Dr. Fuller: *Nothing is more playful than a young cat, nor more grave than an old one....Wanton kitlins may make sober old cats.*

Tennyson: *When cats run home and light is come..../ Alone and warming his five wits,/ The white owl in the belfry sits.*

* * * * * * *

Poe: *All that we see or seem/ Is but a dream within a dream.* **(Tennyson:** *Dreams are true while they last.)*

Hippocrates: *The brain is the interpreter of consciousness.*

Wright: *...the process of the universe is cyclic, not endlessly evolutionary.* **(Montaigne:** *The world is an eternal seesaw.)*

Shaftesbury: *Pleasure and pain, beauty and deformity, good and ill, seemed to me everywhere interwoven.*

Sherrington: *The whole story is not just chemistry and physics. There is a final cause at work....no detail is forgotten, even to the criss-cross hairs at entrance to a cat's ear which keep out water and flies....*

Marvell: *Self-preservation, Nature's first great law.*

Dixon: *Every animal, like ourselves, acts teleologically, that is, with a purpose in its doings.*
   We are partakers in a gigantic lottery [of genes and chromosomes]....

Unknown: *Success is not always final. If you build a better mousetrap, nature will breed a smarter mouse.*

Addison: *Is it not wonderful that the love of a parent...should last no longer than is necessary for the preservation of the young?*
   Providence furnishes materials, but expects that we should work them up ourselves.

Aurelius: *Nothing happens to any man which he is not framed by nature to bear.*

St. Augustine: *Miracles are not contrary to nature, but only contrary to what we know about nature.*

Pythagoras: *Nature has given us no knowledge of the end of things.*

Pliny the Elder: *It is the nature of man to yearn for novelty.*

Dryden: *All objects lose by too familiar a view.*

Danish proverb: *There is no day so holy that the pot refuses to boil.*

Africanus: *...harmony with Nature and obedience to her laws.* (**Bacon:** *...we cannot command nature except by obeying her.*)

Hopkins: *Whatever is physiologically right, is morally right; and whatever is physiologically wrong is morally wrong.*

Swift: *Things refuse to be mismanaged long.*

Lucan: *The earth takes back anything which it has brought forth.*

Dean Inge: *...nature takes away an organ [muscles, brains] which is not used.*

Emerson: *Society acquires new arts and loses old instincts.*

* **Goethe, on Nature:** *Those who trust in her she hugs to her bosom like a child. (***Wordsworth:** *Knowing that Nature never did betray/ The heart that loved her.)*
*   *She seems to have built everything on individuality and cares nothing about individuals. (***Tennyson:** *So careful of the type she seems,/ So careless of the single life.)*
*   *Her show is ever new because she creates ever new spectators.*

Thoreau: *It appears to be a law that you cannot have a deep sympathy with both men and Nature.*

MAN vs NATURE

Holmes: *A goose flies by a chart which the Royal Geographical Society could not mend.*

Bacon: *...the breath of flowers is far sweeter in the air...than in the hand...*

G. Herbert: *The tree that God plants, no wind hurts it.*

Blake: *The tree which moves some to tears of joy is in the eyes of others only a green thing which stands in the way.*

Thoreau: *We have not learned by experience the consequence of cutting off the forest. [But we will!]*

Byron: *High mountains are a feeling, but the hum/ Of human cities torture.*

Varro: *God made the country and men made the cities.*

Latin proverb: *A great city, a great solitude.* (**Unknown:** *City: a large community where people are lonesome together.*)

Gibbon, on London: *Crowds without company, and dissipation without pleasures [cf.* **Emile Durkheim's** *concept of anomie: lack of purpose and values]*

Hubbard: *A city is no place for children - nor grown people either.*

Arnold: *...this strange disease of modern life,/ With its sick hurry, its divided aims....*

Emerson: *How is it people manage to live on in large cities,- so aimless as they are?* (**Unknown:** *The supreme product of civilization is people who can endure it.*)

Plutarch: *We are more sensible of what is done against custom than against Nature.*

Emerson: *The history of man is a series of conspiracies to win from Nature some advantage without paying for it.*

Jackson: *The Great revolution of the future will be Nature's revolt against men. [Climate change?]*

Spengler: *The fight against Nature is hopeless and yet - it will be fought out to the bitter end.*
   ...every discovery contains the possibility and <u>necessity</u> of new discoveries, every fulfilled wish awakens a thousand more, every triumph over Nature incites to yet others. The soul of this beast of prey is ever hungry, his will never satisfied....All things organic are dying in the grip of organization. An artificial world is permeating and poisoning the natural.... (**Byron:** *Man marks the earth with ruin.* **Marquis:** *It won't be long now/ man is making deserts of the earth.*)
   ...utility, not beauty; quantity, not quality; power, not mankind.

MAN the PREDATOR

Firdusi: *All know their kind, but hapless man alone/ Has no instinctive feeling for his own.*

Hugo: *Beasts belong to God, but stupidity to man.*

Lucretius: *The snake, when touched by man's spittle, perishes and gnaws itself to death.*

Goldsmith: *Brutes never meet in bloody frey,/ Nor cut each other's throats for pay.* (**Sanford:** *One crow never pulls out another's eyes.*)

Cowper: *Detested sport,/ That owes its pleasures to another's pain.* (**Unknown:** *Hunting leads to diminished sensitivity.*)
  ...the man who needlessly sets foot upon a worm.

Blake: *A robin redbreast in a cage/ Puts all Heaven in a rage.*

RELIGION

Santayana: *Religion is an interpretation of the world....*

Emerson: *Religion is the relation of the Soul to God....* (**Krause:** *Religion is man's struggle for union with God.*)

Bacon: *Our humanity were a poor thing but for the divinity that stirs within us.*

Lord Herbert: *...there is a universal natural religion which characterizes all mankind....*

Dixon: *...the longing of the spirit, which is the essence of all religions....*

Santayana: *...spirituality is universal, whatever churches may be.*

Rilke: *Religion is not knowledge but a direction of the heart.* (**Dean Inge:** *Religion is caught, rather than taught.*)

Jerrold: *Religion's in the heart, not in the knees.*

Wilde: *It is tragic how few people ever possess their souls before they die.*

Seneca: *Worship does not consist in slaughtering fattened bulls....but in a will that is reverend and upright.*

Boileau-Despréaux: *There is but one road to lead us to God - humility.*

Plato: *To find the Father and Maker of this universe is a hard task; and when you have found him, it is impossible to speak of him before all people.*

Thoreau: *What is religion? That which is never spoken.*

Emerson: *God enters a private door into every individual.* (**Hugo:** *Every man is a book in which God himself writes.*)

Khan: *Belief cannot be taught, it cannot be learned; it is the grace of God. To affirm a belief is one thing; to realize belief is another.*

Koran: *None can have faith except by the will of Allah. Allah misleads whom He will, and guides whom He pleases.* (**Pascal:** *Faith is a gift of God.*)

Paine: *Every national church or religion has established itself by pretending some special mission from God, communicated to certain individuals....as if the way to God was not open to every man alike. The true revelation is the universe we behold....We can know God only through His works.*

Whichcote: *If you say you have a revelation from God, I must have a revelation from God too before I can believe you.*

Carlyle: *Wonder is the basis of worship.*

Lucretius: *True piety is this: to contemplate with mind serene the whole.*

Santayana: *My atheism, like that of Spinoza, is true piety towards the universe and denies only gods fashioned by men in their own image, to be servants of their human interests.*
   ...the infinity which moves us is the sense of multiplicity in uniformity.

Einstein: *I am a deeply religious man....I shall call it cosmic religious feeling.*

Mencken: *I am anything but a militant atheist....Brahms moves me far more powerfully than the holy saints.*

Dewey: *Militant atheism is also affected by lack of natural piety. The ties binding man to nature....*

Rousseau: *...my worship consisted rather of wonder and contemplation than of petitionary prayer. I can understand how it is that city-dwellers, who see only walls and streets and crimes, have so little religion.*

R. Cecil: *A contemplative life has more the appearance of piety than any other.*

Venning: *[A truly religious philosopher] in the glass of things temporal, sees the image of things spiritual.*

Whichcote: *Good men spiritualize their bodies; bad men incarnate their souls.*

Quarles: *Be wisely worldly, be not worldly wise.*

Lord Herbert: *The true religion is a religion of reason [natural religion].*

Proverb: *A good life is the only religion.*

Proverb: *Religion is the best armor but the worst cloak.*

Unknown: *Religion is institutional, spirituality is personal.*

Conrad: *God is for men and religion for women.*

Hugo: *I'm religiously opposed to [institutional] religion.*

Hume: *The primary religion of mankind arises chiefly from an anxious fear of future events.*

G. Eliot: *...all men needed the bridle of religion, which, properly speaking, was the dread of the hereafter.*
Burke: *Superstition is the religion of feeble minds.*

Dewey: *Religion has lost itself in cults, dogmas and myths.*

Emmons: *The more men have multiplied the forms of religion the more vital Godliness has declined.*

Zangwill: *'Ceremony is the casket of religion.'*

Franklin: *...vital religion has always suffered when orthodoxy is more regarded than virtue....*
How many observe Christ's birthday. How few of his precepts! 'Tis easier to keep holidays than commandments.

Dr. Fuller: *Religion without piety has done more mischief in the world than other things together.*
Much religion, but no goodness.

Swift: *We have just enough religion to make us hate, but not enough to make us love one another.*

Emerson: *If I know your sect I anticipate your argument.*
Theological problems never presented practical difficulty to any man....
Preaching comes out of the memory, and not out of the soul....
*(***Unknown:*** *Rigorous thought is suspect in the church.)*

Hafiz: *My heart is struck with amazement at those bold-faced/ Preachers, who, of what they say in the pulpit practice so little.*

Thoreau: *The preachers and lecturers deal with men of straw, as they are men of straw themselves.*
They have nothing to do but sin, and repent of their sins....It is a world full of snivelling prayers....

Hubbard: *We are not punished for our sins, but by them.* (***Proverb:*** *Every sin brings its punishment with it.)*

Young: *Forgive his crimes, his virtues too.*

Dixon: *To save morality men will deny the plainest facts....*

Why spend yourself in labour for successors who will render you no thanks, or strive after a heaven of which you have no information?

What sort of God is that who creates a world from which man requires to be saved? He is to save us, it seems, from himself.

Dewey: *The ideal of universal brotherhood professed by religions like the Hebrew and Christian is inconsistent with the doctrine distinguishing between those who are damned and those who are saved....*

Montesquieu: *There has never been a kingdom given to so many civil wars as that of Christ.*

Koran: *The Jews say the Christians are astray, and the Christians say it is the Jews who are astray. Yet they both read the Scriptures. And the Pagans say the same of both.*

Al-Ma'arri: *Moslems, Christians, and Jews -*
All are following the path of error.
In reality humanity is divided into
Intelligent ones who doubt faith
And ignorant ones who are faithful.

*[Similarly, **Bertrand Russell** distinguishes stupid people (who are "cocksure") from intelligent ones (who are "full of doubt".)]*

Selden: *'Search the scriptures.' These two words have undone the world.*

Blake: *Both read the Bible day and night,/ But thou read'st black when I read white.*

Cowper: *Thousands.../ Kiss the book's outside who ne'er look within.*

Santayana: *The Bible is literature, not dogma.*

Hubbard: *A miracle: An event described by those to whom it was told by men who did not see it.*

Edwards: *How many men do you know who let religion interfere with their business?*

Hood: *Alas for the rarity/ Of Christian charity/ Under the sun!*
Isaiah 29:13 (710 BC) *Forasmuch as this people draw near me with their mouth, and with their lips do honour me, but have removed their heart from me, and their fear toward me is taught by the precept of men....*

Reese: *Creeds grow so thick along the way,/ Their boughs hide God.*

Orwell: *...all the smelly orthodoxies which are now contending for our souls.*

Unknown: *Religious contention is the devil's harvest.*

Hubbard: *...theology is a clutch for power. [or wordmongering]*

Spencer: *While the fear of the living becomes the root of political control, the fear of the dead becomes the root of religious control.*

Maugham: *What mean and cruel things men can do for the love of God.*

W. James: *[In holy wars] Piety is the mask, the inner force is tribal instinct.*

Dryden: *We are glad to have God on our side to maul our enemies,/ When we cannot do the work ourselves.*

Chesterton: *...Christianity, which always forbade war and always produced wars [about small points in theology].*

Lowell: *...men burnt men for a doubtful point,/ As if the mind were quenchable with fire....*

Cowper: *Fanaticism, the false fire of an overheated mind.*

Burke: *Religious persecution may shield itself under the guise of a mistaken and over-zealous piety.*

Pope: *For Modes of Faith, let graceless zealots fight....*
The worst madness is a saint run mad.
In hope to merit Heaven by making earth a Hell.

Scott: *...serving the devil for God's sake.*

Proverb: *The nearer the church, the farther from God.*

Defoe: *Wherever God erects a house of prayer,*
The Devil always builds a chapel there;
And 'twill be found, upon examination,
The latter has the largest congregation.

Lucretius: *...this is done for pomp and arrogance/ Rather than deep belief.*

Hood: *Nor think I'm pious when I'm only bilious.*

Hubbard: *Christianity is one thing; the religion of the Christ is another.*

Mencken: *...a firm conviction that the christian faith was full of palpable absurdities....[churches] reducing the ineffable mystery of religion to a mere bawling of idiots....theological hocus-pocus is of a routine and monotonous nature.*

W. James: *Churches, when once established, live at secondhand upon tradition....*

Hubbard: *...hand-me-down religions seldom fit.*

Thoreau: *If it were not for death and funerals, I think the institution of the church would not stand longer.*

...feeble efforts are made to Christianize the natives before they are all exterminated....

Emerson: *...Paganism hides itself in the uniform of the Church.*

Santayana: *Christianity was paganized by the early Church...a mixing of pagan philosophy and ritual with the Gospel....the question between Christians and pagans amounted simply to a choice of fanaticism.... The people could change their gods, but not the spirit in which they worshipped them....*

Zangwill: *Scratch the Christian and you find the pagan - spoiled.*

FAITH

Sherwood Eddy: *Faith is not trying to believe something regardless of the evidence. It is daring to do something regardless of the consequences.*

Polybius: *On any occasion when one can discover the cause of events, one should not resort to the gods.*

St. Gregory: *Faith has no merit where human reason supplies the proof.*

Lange: *Religious ideas are valid as supplements to empirical reality.*

Thoreau: *There is no creed so false but faith can make it true.*

Unknown: *Faith can't be taken on trust.*

Hülsemann: *Faith is not belief without proof, it is trust without reservation.*

Job 13:15 (350 BC) *Though he slay me, yet will I trust in him. [What*
* *else _can_ we do?]* (**Goethe, on Nature:** *She brought me hither, she will see me out. I trust her. She will not repudiate her work.* **Emerson:** *All I have seen teaches me to trust the Creator for all I have not seen.* **Mencken:** *The most satisfying and ecstatic faith is almost purely agnostic. It trusts absolutely without professing to know at all.)*

Hodge: *Faith must have adequate evidence, else it is mere superstition.*

Ellis: *A man must not swallow more beliefs than he can digest.*

Nietzsche: *If a man have a strong faith he can indulge in the luxury of scepticism.*

Barth: *Faith is never identified with piety.*

* Editor's translation

Hilty: *One can achieve a happy life only by accepting whatever happens as though from God's hand, not worrying much and going only through open doors.**

Sir Arthur Conan Doyle: *Several incidents in my life have convinced me of spiritual interposition - of the promptings of some beneficent force outside ourselves which tries to help us when it can.*

Terence: *How often things come by the merest chance, which we dared not even hope for.*

Cleanthes: *Faith leads the willing,/ drags the unwilling.*

Newman: *Keep thou my feet: I do not ask to see/ The distant scene; one step enough for me.*

Billings: *Faith is the soul riding at anchor.*

Quarles: *The way to be safe is never to be secure.*

Proverbs 27:1 (350 BC) *Boast not thyself of tomorrow; for thou knowest not what a day may bring forth.*

Dr. Fuller: *If you leap into a well, Providence is not bound to fetch you out.*

Plautus: *Nuts are given us but we must crack them ourselves.*
(J.G. Holland: *God gives every bird its food, but does not throw it into the nest.)*

Proverb: *Where one door shuts, another opens.* **(Irish variant:** *God never shuts one door but he opens another.)*

Romans 8:28 *And we know that all things work together for good for them that love God....*

* Editor's translation

Psalms 34:18 (250 BC) *The Lord is nigh unto them that are of a broken heart, and saveth such as be of a contrite spirit.* *(**Arabic proverb:** God looks after the friendless.)*

Thos. Adams: *Man's extremity is God's opportunity.*

Proverb: *God shapes the back for the burden.*

Latin proverb: *From God, not from chance.* *(**Proverb:** Providence directs the dice.)*

Athenaeus: *Live in today not for today* *(**Madame Swetchine:** The only true method of action in this world is to be in it, but not of it.)*

de Witt: *Be careful of health, careless of life.*

Haldane: *I've never met a healthy person who worried much about his health, or a good person who worried much about his soul.*

Dewey: *To me faith means not worrying.*

Collier: *Patient waiting is often the highest way of doing God's will.*

Conrad: *...the proper wisdom is to will what the gods will.* *(**Proverb:** Will is the cause of woe.)*

Pythagoras: *Do not pray for yourself; you do not know what will help you.*

Avila: *More tears are shed over answered prayers than unanswered ones.*

Hugo: *Certain thoughts are prayers.* *(**Thos. Brooks:** God hears no more than the heart speaks.)*

H. More: *Prayer is not eloquence, but earnestness...the feeling of [helplessness]. (***Unknown:*** ...a deep-felt need is a prayer in itself.)*

St. Matthew 6:8 *...your Father knoweth what things ye have need of, before ye ask him.*

6:25 *Take no thought for your life, what ye shall eat....Is not life more than the raiment?*

GOD

W. James: *...order and disorder, as we now recognize them, are purely human inventions....by choosing, one can always find some sort of orderly arrangement in the midst of any chaos....There are in reality infinitely more things 'unadapted' to each other in this world than there are things 'adapted'; infinitely more things with irregular relations than with regular relations between them. But we look for the regular kind of thing exclusively....It will be convincing only to those who on other grounds believe in God already.*

Bacon: *...men mark when they hit, and never mark when they miss, as they do generally also of dreams.*

Berkeley: *...all that art and regularity to no purpose?* (**Milton:** *That power/ Which erring men call Chance.*)

Bacon: *...when the mind beholdeth the chain of [scattered causes] confederate and linked together, it must needs fly to Providence and Deity.* (**H. More:** *The mind that knows not what to fly to, flies to God.*)

Hume: *The whole frame of nature bespeaks an intelligent author... Everything is adjusted to everything. One design prevails throughout the whole.* (**Voltaire:** *The harmony of the spheres reveals a cosmic mind.*)

Taylor: *What can be more foolish than to think that all this rare fabric of heaven and earth could come by chance, when all the skill of art is not able to make an oyster.*

Emerson: *Thus astronomy proves theism but disproves dogmatic theology.* (**Young:** *An undevout astronomer is mad.*)

Van Loon, at the Grand Canyon: *I came here an atheist, and departed a devout believer.* (**Goldsmith:** *Fools, who came to scoff, remained to pray.*)

J.G. Holland: *God pity the man of science who believes in nothing but what he can prove by scientific method.*

Bancroft: *Atheism is the folly of the metaphysicians, not the folly of human nature.*

Miller: *The footprint of the savage in the sand is sufficient to prove the presence of man to the atheist who will not recognize God though his hand is pressed on the entire universe.*

Santayana: *...whoever it was that searched the heavens with his telescope and could find no God, would not have found the human mind if he had searched the brain with a microscope.*

Chesterton: *...the more complicated seems the coincidence, the less it can be coincidence.*

Shelley: *It is easier to suppose that the universe has existed from all eternity than to conceive a Being beyond its limit; capable of creating it.*

Spinoza: *...God and nature cannot be separated....*

Lamartine: *God is but a word invoked to explain the world.* (**Cicero:** *God is inconceivable.*)

Trench: *The noise is so great one cannot hear God thunder.*

Seneca: *Nothing comes to pass but what God appoints.* (**Proverb:** *Man proposes, God disposes.* **R. Cecil:** *Duties are ours, events are God's.*)

Tryon Edwards: *All things are ordered by God, but his Providence takes in our agency as well as his own sovereignty.*

Euripides: *We must obey the gods, whatever those gods be.* (**Aquinas:** *We know of God that he is but not what.*)

Browne: *I fear [reverence] God, yet am not afraid of him.*

Roux: *God often visits us, but most of the time we are not home.*

Kempis: *God walks with the humble; he reveals himself in the lowly....*

Staël: *Enthusiasm signifies 'God in us!' [Literally, "possessed by a god"]*

Emerson: *Internal evidence outweighs all other to the inner man.*
(**Young:** *By night an atheist half believes in God.*)

Malebranche: *God is the home of the mind, just as space is the home of the body.*

von Arnim: *Self-reliance is reliance on God.*

Young: *A God all mercy is a God unjust.*

Emerson: *If God is good, why are any of his creatures unhappy?*
(**Maugham:** *Evil is as direct a manifestation of the divine as good.*)

Dryden: *Virtue in distress and vice in triumph,/ make atheists of mankind.*

Diogenes: *The way to heaven is alike in every place.* (**Burton:** *All places are distant from heaven alike.*)

Isaiah 66:1 (710 BC) *Thus saith the Lord, The heaven is my throne, and the earth is my footstool: where is the house that ye build unto me? and where is the place of my rest?*

I Kings 8:27 (600 BC) *But will God indeed dwell on the earth? behold, the heaven of heavens cannot contain thee, how much less this house that I have builded?*

Forster: *Beyond the sky must not there be something that overarches all the skies....Beyond which again...?*

NEW TESTAMENT COMMENTARY: TWO INTERPRETATIONS

Matthew 21:12 *Jesus entered the temple....overturned the tables of the money changers....*

I Timothy 6:10 *For the love of money is a root of all kinds of evil.*
6:7 *For we brought nothing into the world, and we can take nothing out of it.*

I Corinthians 4:7 *What do you have that you did not receive?*

Mark 8:36 *'What good is it for a man to gain the whole world, yet forfeit his soul?'*
10:23 *'How hard it is for the rich to enter the kingdom of God!'*
12:44 *'They all gave out of their wealth; but she, out of her poverty, put in everything - all that she had to live on.'*

COMMENT: Christ's battle against materialism.

John 6:27 *Do not work for food that spoils, but for food that endures....*

Matthew 6:19 *'Do not store up for yourselves treasures on earth, where moth and rust destroy, and where thieves break in and steal.'*
6:21 *'For where your treasure is, there your heart will be also.'*
6:33 *'But seek first his kingdom...and all these things will be given to you as well.'*

COMMENTS: Spirituality is the antidote to materialism: '...a man's life does not consist in the abundance of his possessions.' **(Luke 12:15)**

Matthew 6:34 *'Therefore do not worry about tomorrow, for tomorrow will worry about itself. Each day has enough trouble of its own'*

COMMENT: An early version of "One day at a time."

Luke 12:22 *'...do not worry about your life, what you will eat; or about your body, what you will wear.'*
12:23 *'Life is more than food, and the body more than clothes.'*
12:25 *'Who of you by worrying can add a single hour to his life?'*
12:26 *'Since you cannot do this very little thing, why do you worry about the rest?'*

COMMENT: *Why indeed? Worry is toxic as well as useless.*

Luke 21:34 *'Be careful, or your hearts will be weighed down with dissipation, drunkenness and the anxieties of life, and that day will close on you unexpectedly like a trap.'*

Mark 4:19 *'...the worries of this life, the deceitfulness of wealth and the desires for other things come in....'*

COMMENT: *How timely this all sounds! We unnecessarily complicate our lives and then reap what we sow. The evils we bring on ourselves are hardest to bear.*

Matthew 24:11 *'...many false prophets will appear and deceive many people.'*
23:3 *'...they do not practice what they preach.'*
7:15 *'They come to you in sheep's clothing, but inwardly they are ravening wolves.'*
7:16 *'By their fruits you will recognize them.'*
23:28 *'...on the outside you appear to people as righteous but on the inside you are full of hypocrisy and wickedness.'*

Mark 12:40 *'They devour widows' houses and for a show make lengthy prayers.'*

Matthew 23:5 *'Everything they do is done for men to see. ....'*
6:5 *'Hypocrites love to pray standing in the synagogues and on the street corners to be seen by men.'*

Matthew 6:2 *'So when you give to the needy, do not announce it with trumpets, as the hypocrites do....'*
23:25 *'...you hypocrites! You clean the outside of the cup and dish, but inside they are full of greed and self-indulgence.'*
23:24 *'You blind guides! You strain out a gnat but swallow a camel.'*
23:4 *'They tie up heavy loads and put them on men's shoulders, but they themselves are not willing to lift a finger to move them.'*
6:17 *'...they think they will be heard because of their many words.'*

COMMENTS: *Sound familiar? Has anything changed?*

II Corinthians 9:7 *...God loves a cheerful giver.*

COMMENT: *Paul presumes to speak for God, but the slogan has long been usurped by churches for public fundraising.*

Matthew 26:41 *'The spirit is willing, but the body is weak.'*

I Peter 2:11 *...sinful desires, which war against your soul.*

Galatians 5:17 *...the sinful nature desires what is contrary to the Spirit.... They are in conflict with each other, so that you do not what you want.*

COMMENT: *"I see the right, and approve it, too*
Condemn the wrong, and yet the wrong pursue."
(Ovid, 43BC - 17AD)

I Corinthians 15:33 *Do not be misled: 'Bad company corrupts good character.'*

COMMENT: *"Character is habit long continued."*
(Plutarch, 46 - 120 AD)

Matthew 26:52 *'...all who draw the sword will die by the sword.'*

COMMENT: *Because violence perpetuates itself.*

Matthew 7:13 '...wide is the gate and broad is the road that leads to destruction, and many enter through it.'
7:14 'But small is the gate and narrow the road that leads to life, and only a few find it.'
24:12 'Because of the increase of wickedness, the love of most will grow cold....'

Mark 13:8 'Nation will rise against nation, and kingdom against kingdom. There will be earthquakes in various places and famines.'

I Peter 4:7 The end of all things is near.

COMMENT: Is Global warming moving us ever closer to end times?

Mark 1:15 'Nothing outside a man can make him "unclean" by going into him. Rather, it is what comes out of a man that makes him "unclean".'

COMMENT: "...nothing is unclean in itself." (**Romans 14:14**)

Mark 2:27 'The Sabbath was made for man, not man for the Sabbath.'

COMMENT: Rules (and material things) are good servants but bad masters.

John 8:7 'If any of you is without sin, let him be the first to throw a stone at her.'

COMMENT: Yes. But what is sin anyway?

Mark 7:6, quoting Isaiah 'These people honor me with their lips, but their hearts are far from me.'
7:7 'They worship me in vain; their teachings are but rules taught by men.'

Ephesians 4:14 *....blown here and there by every wind of teaching and by the cunning and craftiness of men in their deceitful scheming.*

COMMENT: Has anything changed?
Mark 4:12 *'...they may be ever seeing but never perceiving, and ever hearing but never understanding; otherwise they might be forgiven!'*
[Isaiah 6:10 has "and be healed" for "forgiven."]
4:17 *'But since they have no root, they last only a short time.'*
[The King James Bible has"roots in themselves."]

COMMENT: No spiritual depth. Has anything changed?

Romans 14:5 *Each one should be fully convinced in his own mind.*

COMMENT: Well said!

Matthew 12:33 *'...out of the overflow of the heart the mouth speaks.'*

COMMENT: Well said!

Matthew18:13 *'...unless you change and become like little children, you will never enter the kingdom of heaven.'*

John 3:3 *'...no one can see the kingdom of God unless he is born again.'*
[Or: "born from above"]

Hebrews 11:6 *[God] rewards those who earnestly seek him.*

Luke 17:21 *'...the kingdom of God is within you.'*

COMMENT: Humility, a humble heart, are the only path to God.

Romans 8:28 *And we know that all things work together for good to them that love God....*

COMMENT: True in my experience, even if "Nature" were substituted for "God!"

Matthew 12:48 *'Who is my mother and who are my brothers?'*
12:49 *Pointing to his disciples, he said, 'Here are my mother and my brothers.'*

COMMENT: *Kinship of mind trumps kinship of body.*

Luke 12:4 *'...do not be afraid of those who kill the body and after that can do no more.'*

COMMENT: *You can't kill an idea.*

Mark 6:4 *'Only in his hometown, among his relations and in his own house is a prophet without honor.'*

COMMENT: *For the same reason that no man is a hero to his wife.*

Luke 11:17 *'...a house divided against itself will fall.'*
16:13 *'No servant can serve two masters.'*

COMMENT: *Observably true.*

Matthew 29:26 *'...whoever wants to become great among you must be your servant....'*

Luke 14:11 *'...everyone who exalts himself will be humbled, and he who humbles himself will be exalted.'*

Galatians 6:3 *If anyone thinks he is something when he is nothing, he deceives himself.*

COMMENT: *Humility and leadership go hand in hand.*

Romans 14:7 *...none of us lives to himself alone....*

COMMENT: *Because we are social animals. No man is an island.*

I Corinthians 1:20 *Where is the wise man? Where is the scholar? Where is the philosopher of the age? Has not God made foolish the wisdom of the world?*
8:1 *Knowledge puffs up....* **I Timothy 6:20** *...What is falsely called knowledge.*
1:27 *But God chose the foolish things of the world to shame the wise; God chose the weak things of the world to shame the strong.*
1:28 *...so that no one may boast before him.*

COMMENT: *Has not Nature made foolish the false knowledge and hubris of science by avenging herself with climate change?*

* * * * * * *

'...let us reason together....' (Isaiah 1:18)

Matthew 15:24 *He answered, 'I was sent only to the lost sheep of Israel."*

Mark 13:10 *'And the gospel must first be preached to all nations.'*

John 8:12 *'I am the light of the world'*

COMMENT: *Which is it?*

Luke 14:26 *'If anyone comes to me and does not hate his father and mother, his wife and children, his brothers and sisters - yes, even his own life - he cannot be my disciple.'*

COMMENT: *How can this be reconciled with the commandment to love one another?*

Luke 14:33 *'...any of you who does not give up everything he has cannot be my disciple.'*

COMMENT: *Does this suggest monomania?*

Matthew 10:34 *'I did not come to bring peace, but a sword [or, 'division,' **Luke 12:51**].'*
10:35, 36 *'For I have come to "turn a man against his father, a daughter against her mother...a man's enemies will be the members of his own household." '*

COMMENT: No kidding! Strange words from the "Prince of Peace!" And we have sectarianism to bear him out.

John 6:42 *They said, 'Is this not Jesus, the son of Joseph, whose father and mother we know? How can he now say, 'I came down from heaven?'*

COMMENT: Precisely. One may be forgiven for doubting Christ's divinity. After all, if a man came forward today proclaiming himself the son of God, would he not be quickly locked up as a lunatic?

Matthew 27:46 *'...my God, why have you forsaken me?'*

COMMENT: Realizing at last that the depth of his self-delusion could not save him.

John 6:58 *'...he who feeds on this bread will live forever.'*
6:60 *On hearing it, many of his disciples said, 'This is a hard teaching. Who can accept it?'*

COMMENT: Who indeed!

Luke 11:23 *'He that is not with me is against me....'*

COMMENT: Not necessarily. He may be neutral.

John 12:47 *'...I did not come to judge the world, but to save it.'*

COMMENT: Save it from what? Does God's world need saving from himself?

Mark 16:16 *'Whoever believes and is baptized shall be saved, but whoever does not believe shall be condemned.'*

COMMENT: But he said he did not come to judge the world! Besides, belief cannot be forced.

Matthew 20:28 *'...the Son of Man did not come to be served, but to serve, and to give his life as a ransom for many.'*

COMMENT: Why do they need ransoming? They are as God made them, for better or worse.

John 3:16 *For God so loved the world that he gave his only begotten Son, that whoever believes in him shall not perish but have eternal life.*

COMMENT: Aren't we all God's children, with or without eternal life, as the case may be, whether we believe in him or not?

Matthew 5:39 *'Do not resist an evil person. If someone strikes you on the right cheek, turn to him the other also.'*
5:44 *'Love your enemies and pray for those who persecute you....'*

COMMENT: Doesn't work because it goes against human nature.

Matthew 22:39 *'Love your neighbor as yourself.'*

COMMENT: Unrealistic and unnatural.

John 13:34 *'A new commandment I give: Love one another.'*

COMMENT: Love is a feeling and cannot be commanded.

Matthew 6:10 *'[Pray] your will be done.'*

COMMENT: Quite unnecessary. It will be done whether we pray or not.

Luke 11:3 *'Give us each day our daily bread.'*

COMMENT: Do earthly children have to beg for their daily bread?

Matthew 6:8 *'...your Father knows what you need before you ask him.'*

COMMENT: Why then do we ask?

Luke 12:24 *'Consider the ravens: They do not sow or reap...yet God feeds them. And how much more valuable you are than birds!'*

COMMENT: An unwarranted assumption. Consider how much more destructive we are than birds, or any other creature, for that matter!

Mark 9:43 *'If your hand causes you to sin, cut it off.'*

COMMENT: Simplistic. What causes the hand to sin? It is only an agent of the brain. (Islam's sharia law repeats the same error.)

Matthew 21:22 *'If you believe, you will receive whatever you ask for in prayer.'*

Mark 9:23 *'Everything is possible for him who believes.'*

COMMENT: Not always.

Luke 11:9 *'Ask and it will be given to you; seek and you will find; knock and the door will be opened to you.'*

COMMENT: It's not clear what is being offered here. We all seek different things, the only certainty being that he who looks for trouble never misses.

I Peter 5:7 *Cast all your anxiety on him because he cares for you.*

COMMENT: *Good therapy for relieving stress and anxiety, whether one believes in him or not!*

Luke 17:33 *'Whoever tries to keep his life will lose it, and whoever loses his life will preserve it.'*

COMMENT: *Yes. Grim intensity often defeats itself. Some things in life must be left to fate.*

I Corinthians 12:6 *There are different kinds of working, but the same God works all of them in all men.*

COMMENT: *How admirably broadminded! Cuts across all religions.*

Romans 9:18 *...God has mercy on whom he wants to have mercy, and he hardens whom he wants to harden.*

9:19 *But who are you, O man, to talk back to God? 'Shall what is formed say to him who formed it,' "Why did you make me like this?" '*

14:8 *So, whether we live or die, we belong to the Lord.*

COMMENT: *Because the gods made us for sport.*